Strategic Planning:

Using Diamond Eyes

to See the Future

Scott A. Romeo

Strategic Planning 2020, LLC
9221 E. Baseline Road
Ste. A109-109
Mesa, AZ 85209
USA
info@planning2020.com

ISBN-13: 978-0990701705 (THE STRATEGY EXPERT)

ISBN-10: 0990701700

One week before the stock market crash that led to the Great Depression, Yale economist Irving Fischer is reported to have said:

"Stocks have reached what looks like a permanently high plateau."

CONTENTS

H.W. Warner, one of the three original Warner Brothers, was baffled by the idea of non-silent movies, reportedly saying:

"Who in the hell wants to hear actors talk?"

Orville Wright once scoffed at the notion of airplanes traveling long distances. He reportedly commented:

"No flying machine will ever fly from New York to Paris"

1 SETTING THE VISION

Have you ever wondered why so many businesses fail within the first five years? Commercial lenders and Small Business Administration loan officers almost always require entrepreneurs to submit a business plan as part of the loan application process. Still, according to the U.S. Small Business Administration, nearly half of these businesses won't reach the five year milestone.

Venture capitalists usually require a business plan as part of the funding consideration process, but the majority of the companies funded often fail to achieve expected shareholder value because their plans lack the strategies required for success. In addition, it is believed that during the 2007-2009 recession, many venture capital investments were barely earning any meaningful return on investment. How can this be?

The answer may be simple.

> **A business plan often lacks the careful analysis, strategies and tactics that are required to reach the expected financial returns. Instead, they contain goals, not strategies.**

Throughout my career I have written, contributed to, assessed or conducted due diligence on over 2,000 plans: Business and strategic plans, project plans, humanitarian funding plans, etc. I have written plans for small, start-up organizations and plans for billions of dollars. Once, I wrote a plan that was submitted to the Internal Revenue Service and registered as a US$200 million tax shelter. Having worked with companies in the U.S. as well as Southeast Asia on the formation of strategic alliances and joint ventures, I have experienced the value of forming strategies.

Many templates for planning and software packages leave much to be desired. In fact, most strategists can often identify a plan developed from a software package at first glance because it is missing many of the strategic major elements -- mainly, an insightful analysis and specific action-based strategies to be implemented.

Not every company needs a 2,000 page strategic plan, but every company needs a strategic plan.

Early in my career, when helping clients create business plans, I began to concentrate on the implementation aspect of planning and quickly realized that a business plan is mostly a great brainstorming document. In fact, a business plan is little more than a description of a business and the identification of some desired end results, without substantial relevant analysis, strategies and tactics that are needed to achieve those expected outcomes. As a behaviorist, this approach is too theoretical and difficult to implement. It was then that I realized why business plans that were submitted for funding often failed to meet expectations. They identified the end results (goals) without discernable strategies or actions to be implemented.

The title of this book is *Strategic Planning*: *Using Diamond Eyes to See the Future*. The name is significant for two reasons. Prior to the 2007-2009 recession, many organizations had become complacent in their strategic planning. Some executives viewed the annual strategic planning conference as the opportunity to go on a retreat and play golf for the weekend while working on key objectives. The 2007-2009 economic downturn (The Great Recession) illustrates that short-term strategic thinking does not provide enough long-term strategy to overcome the usual economic cycles of business. It also does not provide enough short-term implementation, control and monitoring to ensure successful implementation of tasks and sub-tasks. Yet, changes brought about by technology and mergers and acquisitions have shortened the planning process. According to CNN, the following chart depicts economic downturns since the end of WWII.

Beginning Month	Ending Month	No. of Months
February, 1945	October, 1945	8
November, 1948	October, 1949	11
July, 1953	May, 1954	10
August, 1957	April, 1958	8
April, 1960	February, 1961	10
December, 1969	November, 1970	11
November, 1973	March, 1975	16
January, 1980	July, 1980	6
July, 1981	November, 1982	16
July, 1990	March, 1991	8
March, 2001	November, 2001	8
December, 2007	June, 2009	18

Figure 1

Figure 1 illustrates that fluctuations in the economy are a normal part of a business lifecycle. It also indicates that most economic down-cycles last approximately 11.09 months; therefore, 3-5 year planning may be insufficient to capture the beginning, duration and complete recovery of a cycle. Any long term strategic plan that does not account for an economic downturn may no longer meet industry standard for a valid strategic plan. Assuming a five year or longer cycle without an economic downturn is not realistic forecasting and planning.

Short-term strategies to develop and maintain ongoing shareholder value work well during strong economic times. However, short term thinking often fails to provide the resources required not only to survive economic downturns, but to take advantage of opportunities that might exist as well.

Companies today should be strategically planning for the long-term but operationally planning for the short-term.

This requires long-term strategies that help organizations lead and manage through the down cycles while concentrating on the big picture -- your macro vision and the required long-term strategies and objectives of your organization. It also requires short-term tasks and sub-tasks that are action-based that need to be controlled and monitored during the implementation process.

This book describes a strategic planning process for an organization that needs a strategic plan, but does not want to spend $60,000 or more for its development. It describes a strategic planning process I developed over 20 years of working with strategic plans and facilitating strategy sessions. Most importantly, the plan is behavior-based. Unlike many strategic, business and project plans today, *QuickStart to Strategic Planning™* plans can be implemented, controlled and monitored in real time.

Diamond Eyes

The concept of Diamond Eyes in the title refers specifically to a person with nearly 20/20 vision. Not physical vision, but the vision to see the future – and that is what is required of a strategic planner. Although no one has a perfect view of the future, it is your ability as a strategic planner to see the future direction. This requires specific skills to be able to design strategies and tactics to make your future a reality. To illustrate this concept, the term *Diamond Eyes* is included in the subtitle of this book.

In 2008, while flying back to the United States from a consulting engagement in Southeast Asia, I watched a movie on the plane that was based upon the book *Dive* by Eto Mori. The movie was about The Mizuki Diving Club and its desire to overcome hardships and to have one or more of its divers make the Olympic diving team. At the diving club, there was a young diver trying to make the team and continually improving until one day one of his coaches tells him that he had the potential to be great -- he had **Diamond Eyes**.

In the movie, this term meant the young diver had the ability to envision the complete dive – all the way through the rotations off the diving board and his entry into the water, all before he left the diving platform. He had the vision to see the future - **Diamond Eyes.**

You might be wondering what this has to do with business and strategy. Those individuals who have the ability to see through the day-to-day issues that plague many organizations and the ability to plan through short-term economic cycles can plan strategically. They view the business environment from a systematic or macro perspective and have **Diamond Eyes** and will likely be the ones who become the industry leaders.

The *QuickStart to Strategic Planning*™ process also uses the concept of rapid cognition, as explained in the book *Blink* written by Malcolm Gladwell. Fast-paced, almost instantaneous analysis is often beneficial to the strategic planning process, yet many either dismiss such thinking as intuition or a gut reaction. While one would not want to devise a complete strategic plan completely based upon intuition, there are aspects where a quick analysis can be as beneficial as days or weeks of analysis. This can particularly be useful when conducting a risk assessment or a stakeholder analysis. Thus, I have integrated rapid cognition into the *QuickStart to Strategic Planning*™ process. As a result, I have reduced the amount of time required to create a strategic plan by nearly one-third.

Are there examples of individuals who have **Diamond Eyes**? It is said that Jamie Dimon, the CEO of JP Morgan Chase, saw that the sub-prime mortgage industry was about to collapse and he immediately began to exit that risky line of business – nearly 18 months before the collapse -- while he could still get a return on the portfolio. If this is in fact true, it appears as if Mr. Dimon "saw a vision" and called his VP, who was on vacation, and suggested that Chase immediately begin to sell parts of the portfolio, even if it meant losing short-term revenue to the competition.

I know it is easy to become engaged in the day-to-day issues facing organizations; however, those who have developed **Diamond Eyes** can utilize a systematic approach to planning and thus have a better chance of not only surviving, but thriving.

Thought to Ponder: If you don't have someone with **Diamond Eyes** on your team – find someone.

---

2 DIFFERENCES BETWEEN A STRATEGIC AND BUSINESS PLAN

When asked to explain the differences between a business plan and a strategic plan, there are many. Frankly, I am amazed at the number of organizations who spend so much time designing business plans, only to then discover that a business plan lacks the critical elements for success - strategies.

Most business plans usually lack meaningful analysis, with the exception of some financial modeling with projected revenues for the next few years and a SWOT analysis. Of course, without describing specific strategies, it is difficult to assess the probability of achieving these projections. Many business plans describe a company and what it does (its mission) then jumps to an anticipated outcome or result, such as $10 million in sales in three years. Most business plans contain very few strategic approaches or tactics (the actual behavior) to ensure, for example, that the sales projection can be realistically achieved. In fact, most business plans lack the strategies and tactics that would be required to achieve the desired results.

> **Thought to Ponder**: Ask yourself this question: "If I handed the business plan to someone else to implement, would that person know what to do?"

Seldom, little benchmarking is conducted and a competitor analysis completed in a business plan. It is amazing the number of companies that think they don't have competitors. Too often industry analyses, if provided at all, are insufficient to draw meaningful conclusions, let alone develop a strategy. At best, a business plan could be classified as a "concept document". One would rarely read a business plan and discover strategies and tactics that could be implemented by the organization. Without knowing the strategies and tactics, how can any investor or loan officer ascertain if the end results (usually labeled as "goals" or financial projections) are accurate or even meaningful?

Many business plans include a SWOT analysis (Strengths, Weaknesses, Opportunities and Threats). While it is often referred to as a SWOT Analysis, little to no actual analysis takes place. In fact, SWOT is not much more than a brainstorming activity, and an incomplete one at that. In the early 1970's a second "T" was added to the original model to change the model to SWOTT with the second "T" representing Trends. Today, a SWOTT analysis that does not include Trends is considered incomplete.

If truth be told, It is not until the results of a SWOTT analysis are used to conduct a TOWS analysis (SWOT spelled in reverse) that meaningful strategies can then be developed. Even though TOWS has been around for many years, it is rare to find one in a business plan. It is not until this second step, TOWS – where each item is match-paired with other elements that one can even begin to think about analysis, and then strategy development.

In fact, SWOTT is only step one of a 3-step process but steps 2 and 3 are hardly ever utilized in a business plan and often overlooked in strategic plans. The complete analysis model to analyze strengths, weaknesses, opportunities, threats and trends is as follows:

Step 1: SWOTT analysis: a brainstorming activity to identify strengths, weaknesses, opportunities, threats and trends

Step 2: TOWS analysis: a match-paired comparison

Step 3: Strategy and tactic development

While a business plan may often contain a SWOT analysis, a strategic plan will include the TOWS analysis and the recommended strategies. This is explained in more detail later in the analysis section of the book.

Thought to Ponder: Do you only complete the SWOT brainstorming activity or do you utilize all three steps and analyze the results? Do you use the results to develop strategies? If you only conduct the SWOT portion, your strategic planning time can be better spent in the area of strategy development.

Some business plans include a few identified risks; however, very few risks are numerically assessed, let alone having strategies associated with them. While business plans might include a list of a few risks, strategic plans include not only the identification of each significant risk, but a numerical assessment of each one. This ensures the probability or likelihood that the risk will occur. A contingency strategy for each risk will warrant planning. A risk assessment is discussed in more detail later in this book in the analysis section.

Just a few years ago, the world entertained the possibility of an H1N1 Influenza A outbreak. Most likely less than 95% of the businesses below the Fortune 500 level created meaningful mitigation plans or contingency strategies related to this or any similar event.

The reader might add, but the H1N1 outbreak was not a major event and we would have wasted valuable resources designing management and mitigation plans for something that did not occur. That is likely the same rationale that the companies in The Twin

Towers might have used prior to the 9-11 attack. Why waste time preparing for a terrorist event within the country? After all, most terrorists had historically targeted locations outside of the U.S. The fact that the building was subject to an attack in 1993 should have been an indication that something is likely to occur in the future and management and mitigation strategies should have been prepared. Numerical-based risk assessments are discussed in more detail later in the book.

*A **Stakeholder** is identified as any entity, internal or external, which could affect an organization or be affected by an organization.*

Very few business plans contain a numerically-based stakeholder analysis. Strategic plans should include not only the identification of each major stakeholder, but the potential impact of each stakeholder should be numerically assessed, with management and mitigation and/or contingency strategies designed for those stakeholders who require attention.

Just one stakeholder could have a major impact upon a company. For example, on September 11, 2001, Cantor Fitzgerald, a financial services and brokerage firm located in the Twin Towers of New York City, lost 658 members of its family. Although this is an extreme example, less than 1% of the business plans that I see contain a meaningful, numerically-based stakeholder assessment, with plans.

Most business plans do not adequately assess the bargaining power of suppliers and customers, the threat of new entrants, the threat of substitute products or the competitive rivalry within the industry; whereas almost all strategic plans contain this Five Forces Analysis. Results of the Five Forces Analysis can often be migrated to the stakeholder analysis, the risk assessment and other segments of the strategic plan.

While it is impossible to describe the entire strategic planning process in a book, one of my most popular strategy sessions that I facilitate is sales and marketing. I present some of the content of a session here in order to illustrate strategic thinking that must take place within organizations. From a strategic perspective, most business plans do not reflect the difference between <u>sales</u> and <u>marketing</u>. A "red flag" is when an organizational chart states there is a *Vice President of Sales and Marketing* or a *Director of Sales and Marketing*. These two functions (sales and marketing), are only remotely related in the strategic sense. Sales and marketing require two distinct skill sets rarely found in one individual. These functions should be distributed between two individuals and when they are, these two people will often argue and disagree. Because the sales and marketing module is one of our most popular strategy sessions, I have included various aspects of that module from our QuickStart to Strategic Planning™ materials.

Strategically, marketing is an internal function within an organization and is often considered a cost center. Sales are an external function that generates revenue. The two are strategically linked together via advertising and public relations. Most business plans do not represent the fact that companies simply do not market what they sell at the strategic level. This inability of companies to identify the differences between sales and marketing, a key to revenue generation and return on investment (ROI), often leads to a failed company.

While a business plan often does not account for these sales and marketing differences, a strategic plan allows for not only the distinction between the functions of sales and marketing, but the effective use of marketing strategies to help create sales tactics that in turn generate sales dollars.

Finally, the last major distinction between a business plan and a strategic plan encompasses all of the facets related to strategy development. Business plans almost always describe an end result with little or no specific strategies on how the end result will be achieved. For example, generating $10 million in sales is an end result. You could achieve $10 million in sales through various means, including simply acquiring a company with $10 million in sales, but that may not be what your organization had in mind when you set your goal. This is why you should concentrate less on goals, and more on your strategy development and tactics. It is good practice to study strategic plans posted online by government agencies, non-profits, school districts, colleges and universities, economic groups and others. Under the heading of "Strategy", many of these organizations list goals, without realizing that goals are not strategies, but are outcomes or results they hope to achieve **if** the correct strategies and tactics are implemented. Even more surprising, approximately 15% of the strategic plans reviewed online have no strategies listed at all.

These distinct differences, along with others, will be presented throughout the remainder of the book. Please keep in mind that a strategic plan encompasses evaluating the past, understanding the present and predicting the future. Strategic planning is both an art and a science that require a highly trained strategist with Diamond Eyes.

3 WHERE IT ALL BEGAN

Strategic planning has been around since nearly the beginning of civilization. Over the years, it has evolved from a practice used by the military to a systematic process used by businesses all over the world.

The history of strategic planning dates back to the days of Greek dominance when each of the ten ancient Greek tribes annually elected a "strategos" (who was literally the General of the Army) to head its regiment. "At the battle of Marathon (490 BC), the *strategoi* advised the political ruler as a council. The strategoi gave 'strategic' advice about managing battles to win wars, rather than 'tactical' advice about managing troops to win battles".

In the 1920s, Harvard Business School designed one of the first strategic planning methodologies and in the 1950's, following the lessons learned from World War I and World War II, the strategic planning process advanced to the next level within the military industrial complex. Defense contractors, many being managed by former military personnel, found it easy to transition the strategic planning process from the military to defense contracting companies. Some of those carryovers are still in place today, including the use of the word mission; a term used by troops on their daily pursuits – now used by employees in their daily duties.

As the 1970's and 1980's progressed, managers and consultants incorporated new dimensions into the methodology, such as Five Forces Analysis to expand into the modern industrial arena.

For the past two decades, prior to *The Great Recession of 2007-2009*, strategic planning has centered on a process of mergers and acquisitions in order to create larger organizations to compete on a global scale or to increase shareholder value. My experience has been assisting US companies and their global expansion plans (mainly into Asia). My conclusion is that the M&A approach, as practiced in the U.S., is not always the best way to develop long term-growth. A merger or an acquisition is merely a transaction that increases shareholder value, is often traded from one group to another and no real growth takes place. The hope is that the synergy created by combining two firms will generate additional growth and revenue but that often does not occur. The AOL-Time Warner merger and the Daimler-Chrysler merger are examples of where 1+1 could equal less than 2.

I now advocate organizations change their strategic mindset to one of strategic alliances and joint ventures centered on specific strategic growth. Not only is this approach more beneficial to the long-term growth of the organization, it is instrumental to the growth and development of a national economy as well. Merely shifting shareholder value from one entity to another via a merger or an acquisition does not build long-term, sustainable growth. For organizations seeking global relationships, strategic alliances and joint ventures are more popular than mergers and acquisitions outside of the United States.

There are many definitions of strategic planning. InvestorWords defines strategic planning as, "The process of determining a company's long-term goals and then identifying the best approach for achieving those goals". This is a basic definition that adequately describes what takes place during the strategic planning process, but may place too much emphasis upon goals. My view of strategic planning is:

Strategic planning is the ability to evaluate the past, understand the present and achieve the future.

In my years working with organizations on various aspects of strategic planning, I have observed that many executives have extensive data that allows them to evaluate the past and by conducting a trend analysis, the company can predict what the future might be. However, most leaders have a difficult time understanding the present state of the industry and the competition.

What might strategic planning be like in the future? While no one knows for sure what the future holds, there are some areas in which change is taking place. The recession has caused many organizations to use the strategic plan on a daily basis. Its importance seems to have increased in many organizations and its significance will likely continue to grow. It also appears as if leadership is sharing the strategic plan more throughout the organization than in recent years. Perhaps the need for competitiveness is enhancing while the need for confidentiality is decreasing.

4 DEVELOPING A STRATEGIC MINDSET

Planning strategically is both an art and a science. While no two strategists are likely to agree upon the exact percentage distribution between these two concepts, I would estimate that strategic planning is about 75 - 80% science and 20 - 25% art. While it is the science component (gathering data, studying the competition, analyzing the stakeholders, assessing the risks, etc.) which consumes most of the planning time, it merely sets the stage for the "arts" portion in which data is interpreted and assumptions are made based upon the data.

In other words, any trained and skilled professional can perform the mechanical part of strategic planning, but it is the person with Diamond Eyes who is able to integrate the "arts" aspect into the strategic process. This often determines the difference between the success and failure of your strategic plan. So, while the scientific aspect of strategy development consumes most of the time, it is often that "artistic" aspect of strategy that creates your competitive edge.

There are some fundamental steps in the strategic planning development process as well as additional methodologies to utilize throughout your strategic implementation process. Some analysis of your organization, the industry, the competition and the geographic and demographic areas in which the organization operates must be also considered.

Stakeholders must be analyzed, past trends must be considered and risks must be assessed. Some of this information is historical and can be gathered by a strategic team. Other key elements may require strategy sessions. For example, two competitors may have merged in the past six months or may be discussing a merger today. The impact of these two stakeholders upon your organization may now have changed and these two stakeholders must now be assessed as a single stakeholder. New strategies may be required to compete against them and mitigation and contingencies strategies may need to be developed to counter their moves.

While most organizations can conduct some basic analysis as described above, many often do so through their own "strategic lens". In other words, they view the world through a filter and that filter is based upon their own experiences. This might work if your company is number one in the industry and the world revolves around your company, but this is not the case 99.99% of the time.

In order to think logically and strategically, each member of your organization must have "a strategic mindset".

When most people participate in a strategic planning session, they tend to focus on their own world – that part of the organization that pertains to them because that is their experience. They are inclined to focus on tasks or tactics because that is what they relate to on a daily basis. However, to think strategically, one must first think at the macro or "big picture" level, not the micro or task level. The organization has to be viewed holistically, and not just from an internal perspective. This requires a competitive analysis and industry perspective as well. The whole world does not center around one department or division – but is a culmination of all of the functions of the organization, all working systematically like a well-oiled machine in relation to the external environment.

Unfortunately, each person's view is often compromised by past experiences and individual interpretation of events. I once worked with a gentleman who spent 27 years at a Fortune 500 multinational corporation and when we began working together, this former manager was only able to process topics based upon his past work experience. His experiences were engrained as part of his thinking process. Regardless of the topic, his response usually started with, "at my old company, we did it this way…." There is nothing necessarily wrong with that. However, his view of the world was much smaller when it is based only on that singular view gained by one individual from one organization. In addition, as a top Fortune 500 Company, it had resources at its disposal to implement strategic plans that other organizations could not match. To compare other companies and ideas against his experience was a very narrow focus and he was often unable to see events outside of his past experience.

This holistic perspective is one advantage that external consultants can bring to the strategic planning process. They work with many organizations and their view of the world is not based upon a singular experience, but years of experience. While a consultant might have 1,000 opportunities to work on a strategic plan, an executive may only work on one company plan a year.

Over time, the actions and behaviors of employees become part of the organization. Once that occurs, these actions and behaviors become 'the way we do things around here". In the example above, the former financial manager saw things the way he did because that was his actions and behaviors for 27 years. In other words, a culture is created. That culture might be good, neutral or bad, depending upon the individuals and their actual behaviors. Culture of the organization must be considered as part of the strategic planning and implementation process.

I often asked this former financial manager to work on a project and to let me see a draft as soon as possible. At first, I thought he had terrible time management skills because it would take him a long time to complete tasks. When confronted, he admitted that he really didn't feel comfortable turning in a draft because that wasn't the way things were done at his former organization. He would rather wait and turn in a final deliverable. While that approach might have worked well at a large multinational organization, it did not work well for a smaller company that needed to adapt quickly to change. The culture at his former company dictated his behavior, which reinforced the culture. I had to be careful or his style would become the culture at our organization as well. I quickly learned that he worked best if a draft was provided to him and he was asked to finalize the deliverable.

Suppose an organization has a department in which two of the managers tend to meander in late in the morning, take extra-long breaks and sometimes leave early. If this behavior is not addressed, over time, the employees who report to those managers will notice that there seems to be no consequences associated with time violations. As a result, those employees will embrace the culture of not taking time management seriously. This will ultimately evolve into a culture in which time and time management is not a serious consideration.

What happens if the two managers are replaced? The new managers will have to work hard to change the established culture because employees are likely to continue their practice of arriving late and leaving early until the new management changes the culture. If this occurs, the strategic plan needs to incorporate change management strategies in order to change the behaviors, and ultimately the culture.

At least in the Multinational Corporation and time management examples, there is a consistent culture in place. What happens when members of your organization have different views on what should occur? Have you noticed that people can observe the same events and interpret different conclusions from the same experiences? You only have to look at the current political environment in the United States as an example. I often conduct an exercise in my training classes where everyone is asked to select one of three envelopes, with each envelope having some unknown internal value. Decisions are made based upon experiences of the participants. For example, one person might refuse to select the FedEx envelope because his divorce papers once arrived in a similar envelope but another person in the same session might immediately select the FedEx envelope because her grandmother used to send her birthday and holiday checks in this manner.

Asking everyone on a strategic planning team to evaluate the past, understand the present and predict the future through their own strategic mindset can be a challenge when people can't even agree upon which envelope to select in a training exercise or which political platform is best for their country. That is why a seasoned strategist who is also a highly trained facilitator must lead strategy sessions.

Now you can begin to see how difficult it can be to establish the right strategic mindset. If executive leadership has decided it wants to be aggressive and earn market share away from the competition next year, everyone on the planning committee must have that same mindset. If not, the team might not even select the correct strategies and tactics.

Occasionally, members of the strategic planning committee disagree. More often than not, the members disagree over their perception of the same topic or issue. This is often a case of individual strategic mindset in disagreement with others on the team. Different philosophies, backgrounds and experiences will cause individuals to view the same topic, situations and decisions differently. This is why it is essential to make sure the person facilitating the strategy sessions is not only an experienced strategist, but a certified facilitator as well. If a strategic mindset is created, personal views can often be set aside and the strategic picture of opportunities can become part of the strategic process. This has to be done at the beginning of the first strategy session so all stakeholders recognize the general direction being pursued.

In order to refocus group members who are viewing the same situation differently or arguing over different perceptions or interpretations of the same topic, I have successfully used the following exercise by writing this sentence for everyone to see at the same time:

I didn't say you stole my money!

At first, everyone appears baffled by this simplistic, but perhaps accusatory sentence that now appears before them. I ask what the sentence means and soon receive different interpretations. Even though the sentence is very basic with no word more than five letters and every word common in the English language, the meaning depends upon which word is emphasized when the sentence is read. Read each sentence below while emphasizing the bold and underlined word and then think about the meaning before moving to the next sentence.

<u>I</u> didn't say you stole my money!

I **<u>didn't</u>** say you stole my money!

I didn't **<u>say</u>** you stole my money!

I didn't say **<u>you</u>** stole my money!

I didn't say you **<u>stole</u>** my money!

I didn't say you stole **<u>my</u>** money!

I didn't say you stole my **<u>money</u>**!

After this discussion, we are usually able to refocus the team's efforts to the task while recognizing that each person may have a different mindset and interpretation at any point in time, and we need to assess each situation and agree upon outcomes and move forward. Then, you need to focus on developing a similar mindset centered on the strategic direction for the entire organization. All of this needs to be done without creating The Abilene Paradox environment. *The Abilene Paradox occurs when members of a group collectively agree to pursue a strategic path that none of them wishe to pursue individually. It is the failure to manage agreement.*

One final exercise to develop a strategic mindset is rather different, but can be quite effective at the same time. It is sometimes difficult to get executives to participate in this exercise but for those who do, even they find the results to be surprising.

Each member is assigned to a private breakout room that is equipped with pens, pencils, a whiteboard, flip chart – but NO COMPUTER. Each individual is asked to take a short amount of time, perhaps 10-15 minutes, and have a conversation with himself/herself regarding the organization. In essence, the participant is holding a strategy session with himself or herself as the facilitator, subject matter expert, contrarian and audience member.

Each participant is told to not sit any more than is necessary, but to get up and walk around the room, write on all of the materials that are available and begin strategically talking to themselves about the organization. They are encouraged to draw pictures, diagrams, or flowcharts while they describe to themselves what their organization should look like.

When you talk to yourself, you are nonjudgmental and you do not interrupt; thus allowing the creative energy to just flow. This exercise helps develop a macro, strategic mindset in order to think outside of the box to utilize a systems thinking strategic approach. This approach can be very effective, particularly if utilized near the beginning of the planning sessions to help each member develop his/her view of the organization. Each person has presented and defended the strategy to themselves. This approach can also be effective with problem-solving, decision making and negotiating sessions.

I call these Strategic Soliloquy Sessions™ and the amount of creative energy resulting from these private sessions is often amazing. In fact, some managers and executives walk out of their breakout room looking as if they have just returned from a pilgrimage and they have such new ideas they can't wait to get back to the strategy session to share with the group.

Another interesting characteristic of the strategic mindset is two-dimensional thinking. This characteristic is observed more so in the United States than in Asia or Southeast Asia. Maybe we are too busy in the United States to consider more options or we simply like to narrow our choices down to two, but in most instances, we seem to have two options and both choices are often opposing points of view.

To help illustrate this two-dimensional thinking, one might

visualize the two options on a continuum such as the one shown below. Pay particular attention to the two opposing options that are often available to us as we make decisions (presented and classified in no particular order):

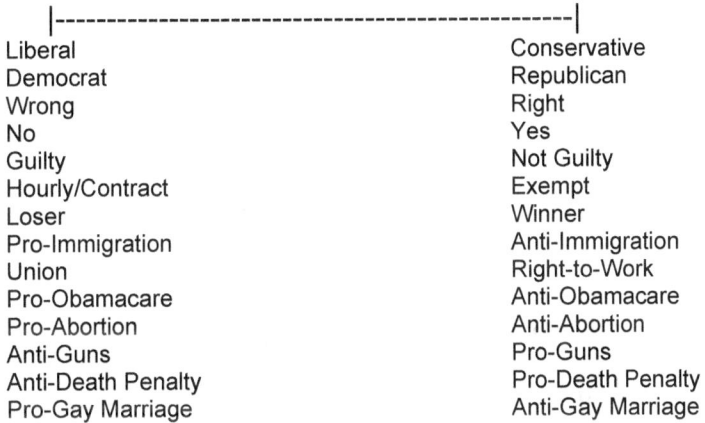

```
|--------------------------------------------------|
Liberal                                Conservative
Democrat                               Republican
Wrong                                  Right
No                                     Yes
Guilty                                 Not Guilty
Hourly/Contract                        Exempt
Loser                                  Winner
Pro-Immigration                        Anti-Immigration
Union                                  Right-to-Work
Pro-Obamacare                          Anti-Obamacare
Pro-Abortion                           Anti-Abortion
Anti-Guns                              Pro-Guns
Anti-Death Penalty                     Pro-Death Penalty
Pro-Gay Marriage                       Anti-Gay Marriage
```

Notice that many of the major decisions we make in life in the US are choices among only two major options, both at opposing ends of the continuum. We may like to vacation on a warm sunny beach while others may want to rest at a mountainous ski resort. One person might work a service job while his neighbor manufacturers products.

With so many opposing views, how can an organization create a uniform strategic mindset so that everyone implements the plan on time and within budget? Hopefully, the session facilitator will help alleviate many of the differences and then it us up to management to manipulate the environment to ensure a successful implementation.

Strategically, you have to consider many options. There are more than two ways to look at any opportunity, problem or decision. Futurist Alvin Toffler, in his famous 1970 book, *Future Shock*, stated that we should at least consider three perspectives. He referred to these three dimensions as: Thesis → Antithesis → Synthesis. You may start with an idea or thesis and someone else may have an entirely different view, an antithesis. By discussing and analyzing each perspective, a new approach, the synthesis of the ideas, can be developed that works for all members of the organization.

Strategic planning requires having the ability to "think outside of the box" and consider other alternatives and options, some of which may never been considered in the industry. That is why an organization needs a strategist with Diamond Eyes – the ability to see what the future might hold.

The goal of this chapter is to encourage you to open your mind and recognize that there are many different perspectives, options, alternatives and decisions that can be made during strategic planning sessions. Using Diamond Eyes, one can look forward and see which options might be best in the short-term as well as long-term. Make sure you have a designated strategist on your strategic planning team or you may be creating strategies and tactics that severely limit the possibilities.

Moreover, if another organization recognizes those same

strategic possibilities, it may take advantage of them and earn market share away from your organization. As the saying goes, "things are often not as they seem" and that is very true. Hiring a key employee away from the competition may cause that person to be a leader in your organization because that person has knowledge about what the competition is doing. Hiring a recent college graduate may be better than hiring the candidate with 10 years' experience because the recent graduate might know current theories and practices taking place rather than what was taught more than a decade ago. It is imperative to think outside the box early on in your planning process. This requires a strategic mindset.

Thought to Ponder: On a scale of 1 to 100, how would you rate yourself on the degree that you view strategic situations from many different perspectives?

"We are not retreating - we are advancing
in another direction."

♦ Douglas MacArthur

5 THE STRATEGIC TIME MACHINE

Strategic planning provides an organization with the unique opportunity to alter time. Do you want to increase sales by $50 million? A Phoenix-based company once told me it wanted to design an intricate marketing campaign, hire external public relations and advertising firms, contract with a call center, train the sales and customer support team and spend the next two years increasing sales. After spending a day with the organization and observing its capabilities I asked the question, "Instead of putting your entire organization through that two-year ordeal, why don't you spend some of your available cash and acquire a company within the industry that already has $50 million in sales?"

Here is what the organization did not realize. Increasing sales by $50 million was a goal or end result or outcome. Leadership skipped the strategy development stage and envisioned the end result - $50 million in sales. Without consideration of various strategies, it selected the first option mentioned by a leading executive with an outgoing personality – a nationwide marketing campaign. Instead of concentrating on the goal ($50M in sales), executives should have been concentrating on the other possible strategies at their disposal. In this case, acquisition strategy - acquiring a competitor - made sense as the most obvious strategy to pursue.

This one question about strategy instead of asking about the goal impacted the entire organization for the next two years. They saved 18 months of valuable time. Amazingly, leadership had not considered that alternative strategies were available because the executive leading the effort had spent many years at another company that grew by launching marketing campaigns each time it needed to grow. To this executive, there were no other strategic choices for growing revenue except launching a nationwide marketing campaign in the hopes of increasing sales. His past experience caused him to create a strategic mindset that offered only one solution. He had only one tool to use in his management toolkit.

One of the benefits of strategic planning is that the planner, to some extent, gets to manipulate and control time. In this case, the time period for growth from 24 months was reduced to 6 months. A competitor was acquired and integrated into the corporate culture within six months and the overall impact to the organization was minimal. For the most part, current employees continued with their day-to-day activities, without rolling out a separate two-year campaign. This strategic decision saved the organization 18 months, removed a potential competitor from the marketplace, and brought in the competition's customers all at the same time. It also allowed the staff at the acquiring company to continue growing the usual side of the business during the acquisition.

The executive for this company was making the strategic mindset mistake discussed in the previous chapter – all options were processed through a filter with the final strategic decision: should we launch a national marketing campaign or not as the only two viable options. Two-dimensional, linear thinking limits the possibilities and causes an organization to make a strategic choice that is perhaps not in the best interest of the firm. This executive's experience and filtering process was causing him to ask the wrong strategic question. He should have been asking, what is the best way to strategically grow this organization? Instead, he was too focused on the goal or outcome of $50 million in additional sales because of his past experience. This process is common in small organizations as well as larger firms. If a strategist is in the room at the time, strategic questions could be asked to guide leadership to consider other available strategic options before selecting a path solely based upon past experience.

When organizations decide to work on their strategic plan, they often begin with: 1) an assessment or analysis of how they have historically performed and 2) then talk about what they are currently doing including issues they are facing and then 3) talk about where they want to go in the future. This often results in either one of two outcomes: a) either the discussion is too narrowly focused and strategic opportunities are not considered because the strategy team is looking at the organization as a continual progression of the past, or b) as the future is discussed, too many ideas and options are discussed and the organization has trouble deciding upon a strategic direction. Neither of these situations is ideal for the strategic planning process. In fact, using either approach is likely to limit the strategic mindset resulting in a mediocre strategic plan.

Strategic planning sessions or writing strategic plans are rarely completed in chronological order, even though most of us usually think chronologically. Using a chronological approach simply does not work well for the strategic planning process. Time exists on a continuum and must be seen as a variable, not a constant. For example, tomorrow is the future, but once tomorrow arrives, it will be the present. And two days from now, what is the future (tomorrow) will then be the past. It is like the Thai language. Thai's do not use verb tense so a Thai might say, "I go to the mall". That could be interpreted as "yesterday, I go to the mall", "right now I go to the mall" or "tomorrow I go to the mall".

While strategic planning might look at the past (for lessons learned and trend analysis) and it might look at what is presently taking place, strategic planning is really about the future. We don't plan for the past and planning for the present should already have been done. So why not start the strategic planning session on that last day of implementing the strategic plan? Describe and define the future from the very beginning and then develop the strategies and tactics that will be required to get there.

Thought to Ponder: Start with the end in mind and your strategy team will be more focused in each of the strategic committee meetings. They know where they are headed.

It has been my experience that most people would rather spend more time and energy trying to influence the future instead of recreating the past. Conducting strategic planning sessions in reverse chronological order, or RCO, allows the strategy team to do just that. Let us dedicate time, effort and resources toward what the team can influence, not spend too much time evaluating the past and spending days discussing trend analyzes. Management can pick up the phone and influence the future, but it is difficult to pick up the phone and change the past.

Begin a strategy session by asking questions similar to:

"Pretend today is the very last day of the successful implementation of this strategic plan; what would you like the organization to look like? What do you hope to achieve or be known for?"

These are very powerful questions. First, it immediately gets everyone thinking not about the past or getting wrapped up in numbers or Excel® spreadsheets for analysis. Instead, the team members immediately begin to consider what the possibilities might be. This can be a particularly powerful session if the team members have already completed the Strategic Soliloquy Session™ mentioned in the strategic mindset chapter of going into a room alone and talking to themselves about what the future might hold.

Second, the response to this statement can then be used as the basis for a vision statement. It describes what the organization wants to be. Once an agreed upon image of the future is developed, that image describes what the organization will be in the future **if** the right strategies are selected, the correct tactics are created and the plan is successfully implemented. It is the vision of the organization.

If a mission statement describes who the organization is and the vision describes what it wants to be, this is a creative way of identifying what the future of the organization will look like. Some teams have a difficult time creating a vision statement because they look at creating the vision statement as a process. It is not, or should not be viewed as an activity; it is the very basis and future of the organization. It evolves. It is where the organization ends up based upon careful planning.

Trying to simplify your corporate vision by merely creating a vision statement, or holding a strategy session does not capture the importance of creating a visual picture of what the organization wants to be. Your vision statement provides an image of the future for every member of your organization. It helps define the parameters of future strategic discussions. The strategic vision should be refined as the strategy sessions evolve. For example, it may not include key areas on which the organization later decides to concentrate, such as being socially responsible.

Some organizations design two vision statements. Because vision statements are often shared with the general public, leadership may not want the competition to know what the organization intends to be in the future. Some organizations create a general vision that is shared with everyone and then a competitive vision statement that is only shared with key internal stakeholders.

Finally, this newly formed vision can drive all future strategy sessions. Employees now know where they are headed. Throughout the remaining strategy sessions, your vision can assist in helping guide strategic thinking, ideas, suggestions, recommendation, and ultimately goals and objectives. If someone begins to suggest ideas that are off track or out of the box, participants can reset the course because they know where they are going every step of the way. The trained facilitator can ask the question "is that going to help lead us toward our vision?" If the answer is no, that topic can be permanently or temporarily tabled.

As already indicated, many strategic planning sessions begin with evaluating the past, understanding the present, and trying to predict the future – all in chronological order. As already stated, this process is flawed. Using a vacation as an analogy, one does not start a vacation by analyzing where s/he went the past three years and how many miles are on the car today and then just start driving without a destination. Usually, the destination – the vision or the end -- is one of the first decisions made. Then the family knows how much money to save and budget, how much time to allocate for the trip, and to make a decision whether to fly or drive, etc.

If you use reverse chronological order with vacations, why would you not use a similar process when planning strategically for your organization? Strategic planning is about the future, not the past or present. While the past and present play a small role, the main purpose of strategic planning is to design a plan for the next year, 3-years or 5-years. Start with the end in mind. The sooner the future can be clearly defined, the sooner the strategic plan can be created and the implementation can begin.

In addition to keeping your team focused, using reverse chronological order also reduces the amount of time required to develop a strategic plan. Because the future is identified early in the process, the objectives, milestones, tasks, and sub-tasks can more quickly and easily be created. This reduction in time can be as much as 25% to 33% using reverse chronological order. This is why it has been integrated into the process I developed, *QuickStart to Strategic Planning™*. Root cause analysis saves the organization valuable resources.

Here is how you might create the right strategic mindset. Early in the strategy session, ask managers and executives to forget about today and pretend it is a certain day, some years in the future, when the strategic plan they are working on could be fully and successfully implemented. This is important because it sets the stage for all participants in the strategy sessions that whatever future they create, must be realistic and attainable. Participants should be able to walk into the office on that date in the future and be able to proclaim, "Today, our vision is achieved!" Therefore, it must be very action or behavior-based, and the organization should be able to control and monitor progress being made toward achieving the vision on a regular basis.

The vision has to be realistic. A product or service being utilized in every household is not realistic. If one household refuses to purchase the product or service, the vision is not achieved. Visions, although futuristic, should be achievable. It is the reason why your team will work diligently to implement the strategic plan over the next 3 to 5 years.

The vision has to have meaning and management has to be able to monitor progress toward achieving the vision. After all, performance evaluations and bonuses may be directly or indirectly tied to reaching the vision. Team members will be striving to achieve that vision on a daily basis. Their sense of fulfillment will come from the accomplishment of reaching that vision. If the vision is too unrealistic, employees will not buy into a theoretical concept they feel is unattainable.

In strategy sessions, participants are asked to close their eyes and describe, in as much detail as possible, what they would like the company to look like on the last day of implementation of the strategic plan. If the executives have already completed a Strategic Soliloquy Session™, they often arrive at this meeting already having formed that image or vision. During this session, collect the end-state picture from the participants in the room and then discuss these various visual pictures as a group. As the discussion continues, certain aspects become apparent and soon the team can design a vision statement and formulate a few objectives to help guide the remainder of the strategy sessions.

After this session is complete, facilitate the remaining sessions in reverse chronological order to today's date and begin to complete the internal and external analysis – past and present. Industry reports are studied, a TOWS analysis and stakeholder analysis are completed, a risk assessment is conducted and the team members are able to see the future, but the present as well. This is followed by the creation of tactics and strategies that lead the organization from where it is today to where it would like to be in the future. Thus, strategic planning is a virtual time machine.

6 IS IT A MISSION OR A VISION?

Many leaders and managers of organizations often confuse the differences between *mission statements* and *vision statements*. Since these are the foundation (along with values) of a business or strategic plan, it is imperative that you not only know the difference, but actually use these tools to advance your organization. Mission and vision statements are not the same and they are not interchangeable.

Mission Statement

From an historical perspective, mission and vision statements have been around for a long time. They are nothing new to the world, just relatively new to the business environment. In fact, these concepts, like many business tools used today, are carried over from the military industrial complex. Military commanders used to (and still do) send their troops on daily *missions*. As part of the preparation, the troops are told the purpose and objective of the maneuver that they are instructed to perform. This mission briefing keeps the troops focused on the short-term tasks associated with the day-to-day activities they are performing – and they go out and successfully complete the mission of the day.

Those organizations supporting the troops with supplies – military contractors such as Boeing or Motorola – are major stakeholders in the military industrial complex. They realize the value of the mission statement and adapt the military mission statement to their organizations. Over time, the rest of the business environment observes the benefits of communicating the mission to the workforce and adopt this tool as part of the regular business and strategic planning process.

Mission statements began as primarily an internal function within organizations in a similar fashion to its use in the military -- it was a way for leadership to communicate to the troops (employees), ***This is who we are and this is what we do*** to help focus on the daily tasks at hand. There was a time when it was believed that you should be able to describe who you are and what you do to anyone riding with you in an elevator – all within about 30 seconds (your elevator speech). Thus, a mission statement describes the current state of an organization including who the organization is and what it does.

Mission statements should be written in the present tense and should convey to the public who the organization is and what it does. If possible, the mission statement should be behavior-based or action-based, meaning it should convey in its mission to the workforce this is what you are doing today.

Here is the mission statement of Zale Corporation in its 2004 Annual Report:

The mission of Zale Corporation is to be the best fine jeweler in North America. Our goal is to develop and market the finest collection of jewelry brands by creating a customer experience that builds lasting relationships and generates superior returns for our shareholders. To achieve this objective, we are committed to educate, motivate and reward our employees to maximize the talents of each individual.

Like many organizations, Zale Corporation's mission statement may not be exactly perfect. It begins; *Zale Corporation is to be....* The statement "is to be" implies sometime in the future; not today. That makes it more of a vision – something it wants to achieve in the future. For example, if one reads, *"my plan **is to be** a professional tennis player"* that generally delivers the message that one is not a professional tennis player today. Since "is to be" implies future-based, it also might deliver the message that Zale is not the finest jeweler in North America at the present time, otherwise, the statement might simply state, *Zale Corporation **is** the best fine jeweler in North America.* By using the term **is to be,**

Zale seemingly has turned its mission statement into more of a vision statement.

The Zale Corporation mission statement also indicates that the mission "generates superior returns for our shareholders". What message does that deliver to the reader? For example, with regard to pricing strategies, does this appear to be an organization that utilizes a low-cost pricing strategy? Does this deliver the message that this organization is a best value provider? Or, does this portion of the statement deliver the message that this might be a high cost provider?

Over time, organizations have learned that the mission statement can also be used as a marketing tool: a means of communicating to external stakeholders. Introducing the mission statement to the outside world might mean that the mission statement needs to be refined in order to deliver the correct intended message. Displaying the mission to the outside world then requires the assistance of your marketing department, legal counsel, consultants, behavioral scientists and other experts who can ensure the correct message is communicated.

I believe U.S. businesses are presently experiencing the third phase or transition of mission statements. Not only is it important to communicate to the world who an organization is and what it does; today, mission statements often instill confidence in the stakeholders that the organization is a good corporate citizen. In the aftermath of Bernie Madoff, Enron, WorldCom and others, organizations now seem compelled to incorporate terms associated with social responsibility into mission statements in order to display to the world that they are good corporate citizens. Consequently, since 1999 many mission statements have been modified to reflect this current trend. Many of those organizations that have not modified the mission statement have incorporated value statements or a code of ethics into their organizations.

Vision Statements

We have already discussed the significance of forming a vision statement earlier in the strategic planning process. We have even considered the importance of launching the strategic planning process with the vision and working in reverse chronological order. Most organizations have created vision statements. As stated earlier, because some vision statements may contain competitive intelligence, not all vision statements are shared with external stakeholders. In fact, because employees can often go to work for the competition, some organizations have elected not to share the strategic vision statement even with the internal workforce. Other organizations create two vision statements: one that is shared with the public that is generic and does not include competitive information and similar to where the industry is headed, and one that is internal to the organization and known mainly to the executive leadership team because it states where the organization intends to be when the plan is successfully implemented. The vision statement for publicly traded companies that are shared usually are generic and reflect the basic, overall direction the industry is headed.

A vision statement has very little to do with the present state of an organization so it is only remotely related to the mission statement. In fact, there may be no relationship at all between the mission statement and the vision statement depending upon the strategies selected by the organization.

For example, the mission at NASA during the 1980's might have been to continue the ongoing maintenance and support of space shuttle missions. Most of the NASA employees and contractors worked on that mission day-to-day. However, the vision of NASA at that same time might have been to advance space exploration by preparing for Mars expeditions. So, the mission at the time was the space shuttle program but the leadership team might have been working on the vision of the organization – Mars exploration.

The vision statement of an organization is usually developed by leadership. Mid-level managers are often frustrated with the communication process with upper management. To management, it seems like the leadership team is not on the same page as they are. That is probably true. In fact, it should be true most of the time. If the leadership team and the management team are working on similar projects together, that is often a red flag. An exception might be a crisis management situation that requires the leadership team to become more engaged in the day-to-day operations for a short period of time.

To illustrate, the mission statement is typically being implemented by management, which is concerned with implementing the day-to-day activities of the organization and controlling and monitoring the progress. The vision that the leader develops today, managers will most likely be implementing weeks, if not months, in the future. The current work of managers today, leadership planned for months ago. And what the leadership team is working on today, managers will be implementing months from now. So, the manager is right – leadership and management are often on two different "time zones" or schedules. Remember strategic planning is like a time machine. Often leadership and management are working in two different time zones. Leadership is working on the vision, while the management team is implementing the mission.

Consequently, whereas the mission statement is written in the present tense, a vision statement is always written in future tense. While a mission statement may include words such as, "we are", a vision statement might include words such as "we will" or "we will be".

When the vision is achieved, it will become the mission statement and a new vision statement will need to be developed. When NASA shifted its efforts and most employees began to work on Mars exploration and the space shuttles were retired, the vision became the mission, and a new vision statement was required.

It is surprising the number of organizations, even large ones, who struggle with the concepts of mission and vision statements. Here are some real-life examples taken from the Internet over time of some mission and vision statements.

Remember, the mission statement is who you are and what you do today and written in present tense and the vision statement is what you want to do or be, perhaps 3-5 years in the future, and written in future tense. Company names have been purposefully omitted.

ABC's Vision: *We will provide customer-valued solutions with the best prices, products and services to make ABC the first choice for home improvement.* Since this is the vision statement for ABC, one can only assume that it presently does not feel as if it provides "customer-valued solutions at the best price" and it hopes to do so in the future. One might also assume that it is not the first choice for home improvement.

DEF must have been unsure of its statement a few years ago when it titled its *Mission/Vision*, which is inaccurate because, as already demonstrated, a mission and a vision are distinctly different. As one reads the statement, it appears to be more of a mission statement that lacked any vision. When this was brought to the attention of leadership at DEF, its response was to remove the statement from the website in its entirety rather than to design a mission and a vision statement. Today, it has developed a socially responsible mission statement that meets industry standard.

GHI states its vision statement as follows: *To become the worldwide leader in retailing.* How will it know the day when leadership comes into the office and can state that it is the worldwide leader that day?

JKL has defined its vision to: *Establish JKL as the premier purveyor of the finest coffee in the world while maintaining our uncompromising principles while we grow.* Do you think JKL has created criteria to know the day it will be the premier purveyor of the finest coffee in the world? When will this vision be achieved?

MNO, when asked, **Does MNO have a mission and a vision statement***?* Responded with just one statement: *MNO! Powers and delights our communities of users, advertisers, and publishers, -- all of us united in creating indispensable experiences and fueled by trust.* One gets the sense that MNO leadership was unsure if it had created a mission or a vision statement and elected to use it for both. In actuality, it is a mission statement by industry standards.

Thought to Ponder: Have you clearly defined the mission of your organization and the vision to where you are headed and shared it with key internal stakeholders?

7 ANALYSIS

HISTOB-PEP™

Many strategic plans are too narrowly focused. One gets the sense that the leadership team enters the strategic planning sessions with a predetermined mindset. Over the years, I have found that many of the analysis tools used for strategic planning are limited in nature. The SWOTT analysis is little more than a brainstorming activity. PEST is a good start but never seems to be comprehensive enough. A Porter's Five Forces Analysis often identifies some critical elements, but seems to be limiting in terms of operational functions.

Out of necessity to provide better consulting services to clients in the realm of strategic planning, I have created a strategic planning analysis process that allows the strategy team to look at the organization, the industry and the competition from nine different perspectives. In 1989, I realized that the two-dimensional model of thinking utilized in the United States was not sufficient for making strategic decisions and I created the HISTOB-PEP™ model. HISTOB-PEP™ is a socio-economic model and an acronym representing the following nine components:

> Historical
> Intellectual
> Sociological
> Technological
> Organizational
> Behavioral
> Philosophical
> Economical
> Political

By looking at strategic situations through these nine different perspectives, leadership is able to view different aspects of their own organization, as well as the competition and the environment in which they operate.

HISTOB-PEP™

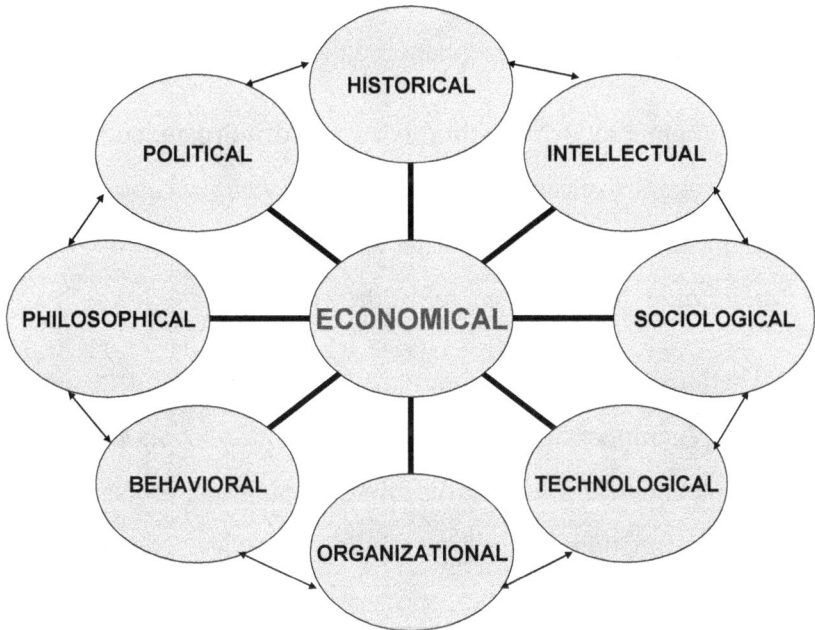

The nine major elements of the HISTOB-PEP™ model are stand-alone functions with interconnected relationships. This means a significant change in one of the nine components would likely have an effect upon at least one, if not all, of the other elements.

Economical appears as the center of the model because it has a two-way relationship. Often, a change in the financial condition of an organization can ultimately affect other parts as well. For example, a decrease in revenue could have an **O**rganizational effect resulting in the layoff of employees, which could have a **S**ociological effect of reducing morale within the organization. On the other hand, increasing the Intellectual capital of the organization could result in better productivity that reduces waste and improve profits, enhancing the Economical component.

Whether an organization is a for-profit organization, a town council, school district, a state college or a nonprofit organization, budgeting is a key element of the strategic planning process. That is why Economical is the center of the model.

The HISTOB-PEP™ model can be implemented as a separate strategic planning model or module during the analysis section or it can be integrated throughout the strategic planning process as each element or function is discussed. While analysis typically occurs early in the strategic planning process; often before strategies are selected and goals are written, I like to utilize the HISTOB-PEP™ model in the strategic planning process to help ensure a comprehensive, congruent strategic plan is being created. While there are many criteria that exist under each of the nine headings, a few are mentioned here to illustrate the modules.

Historical

Although the point has been made that strategic planning is primarily about the future more so than the past, there is some value to understanding the Historical nature of your organization and the industry. Within the organization, if the history presents itself as one in which very little change has occurred throughout the recent past, any significant change could possibly face resistance from key internal stakeholders. This is important to know.

If a strategic plan is being developed that is significantly different from the last strategic plan or what the organization has experienced, this suggests a change management module might need to be integrated into the new strategic plan. Internal stakeholders are often resistant to change if they have worked in an organization that has experienced very little change. A quick review of the history of the organization would help visualize the culture in which the new strategic plan will be implemented. That is important. Designing a strategic plan that won't be implemented by the employees provides little value to the organization. It is important to engage employees in the strategic planning process if significant change is about to occur. This helps reduce resistance during implementation.

It is also important to look at your industry, your competition, your suppliers and strategic partners within the industry, in order to determine how quickly change is taking place within those organizations. An organization's strategic plan does not exist within a vacuum. It has to be created in relation to the aggressiveness of the competition, the pace of change within the industry, the actions of the suppliers and the demands of the customers. An organization might believe that it has created a fantastic strategic plan without realizing that competitor number four and competitor number five are in the midst of merger talks while suppliers in the industry are implementing technology faster than the end users.

Thus, a quick review of your organization and the industry in which it exists has to take place in order to ensure that the strategic plan is congruent with the external environment. Often, reviewing an industry report and reviewing notes an organization may have compiled from a recent association or tradeshow meeting can provide the initial basis for an external review. Whenever possible, I try to get an industry report for a prospective client before the first client meeting. Because industry in the United States is divided into 700 broad categories, it is often difficult to locate a specific report. For example, if a prospective client manufactures hearing aids, the closest industry report might me the manufacturing of medical devices, inclusive of all medical devices made in the United States. The report helps me understand the history of the industry as well as benchmark data and growth projections for the industry over the next 3 years.

Intellectual

We live in a knowledge-based society; therefore, the intellectual capacity or components of an organization are often critical to success. When one thinks of the intellectual property (IP) associated with an organization, the thoughts of copyrights, trademarks, and patents often come to mind. While these are major components and included under the intellectual module, it is also important to remember that the intellectual knowledge of an organization also resides in the minds of the internal stakeholders.

When a new employee is hired, it is important that the intellectual knowledge that was learned by the previous person in that position be shared with that new employee. Mistakes made by the predecessor, as well as accomplishments, should be part of the organizational briefing program. Problems faced by previous employees and how they resolved the problems should be shared with the new employee. There is usually a learning curve associated with the hiring and training of new employees. Don't make your employees continually reinvent the wheel. Provide them with the knowledge to do their job so they can implement their portion of the strategic plan before your competition.

Access to the knowledge database should be provided to new employees. These are the individuals who need to utilize that intellectual knowledge. If it is not shared with them, they have to experience it on their own, just like the previous employee did. Why would an organization want its employees to continually reinvent the wheel each and every time or learn by trial and error?

As your new employees face situations, they should enter those experiences into the knowledge database. The one I use is BrainKeeper (no endorsement implied), and there are others on the market. Software programs such as these can serve as the intellectual knowledge base for the next person who enters this position. When your old employee moves to a different position, it is important that HR conducts an exit interview and captures as much intellectual knowledge as possible. This is entered into the knowledge database to help the next employee make quick decisions and continually implement your strategic plan.

It is important to recognize the source of intellectual knowledge. New hires just graduating from college often know new techniques, models and processes that can be used within your organization. This is one reason why organizations hire college graduates. They often know the latest techniques, particularly related to technology. New hires coming from the competition often know different and sometimes better ways to do things within the organization. Their knowledge base should be seriously considered as long as confidential and proprietary information is not disclosed. This is why it is important for organizations to have a healthy attrition rate. Management expects a certain percentage of the workforce to quit each year. The industry average rate of employee turnover is usually considered the healthy attrition rate. Adapting the strategic plan to reach attrition goals ensures new ideas and skills enter the organization. Organizations need new ideas, and those new ideas often come from employees hired right out of college or away from the competition.

In addition to all of the intellectual property that your organization creates over time, it also has intellectual capital, residing in the minds of your employees. Helping to solve problems faster, finding ways to improve productivity, discovering shortcuts to be more efficient, or learning new ways to be more effective can provide a competitive advantage to your organization. This competitive edge can result in an increase in revenue and ultimately, an increase in market share. These ideas need to be documented and included in the knowledge base of your organization.

It is important to recognize that capturing the intellectual knowledge within an organization is not a cost center; although it may seem like it at the time. One piece of knowledge shared with an employee at a critical time can often make a difference in a project being completed on time and on budget. Creating a knowledge base should be viewed as an investment, not a cost center. It is important enough to be included in the strategic plan of your organization.

Finally, Intellectual also includes the skills or skill sets of the individuals within your organization. It is unlikely that the employees today possess the skills necessary to achieve a 5-year vision. As your strategic plan is implemented, how will your employees acquire the skills essential to implement the plan, achieve the vision and remain competitive? Strategically, should your organization dedicate more resources toward training and development or should you ask employees to assume more of the responsibility? Should your organization work to create a higher employee attrition rate in order to hire new employees with the required skills to begin to work immediately? Should your organization consider outsourcing (one of the strategies discussed later in this book) some functions or utilize contract employees to obtain the necessary skills to take your organization to the next level?

Sociological

The social environment within an organization is often critical to the implementation of the strategic plan. In some areas, you may need to take responsibility and in other areas, a team effort may be required. The social environment is influenced by your leadership and created by all of the internal stakeholders.

The culture of your organization is part of its **S**ociological framework. Too often some cultures within organizations hamper the implementation of the strategic plan. Low morale is often a result or long-term effect of a negative culture.

In order to manage the social environment, culture must be defined. The culture of an organization is created over time. It is not created overnight and it is not created by the leadership team. While leaders and executives within the organization might heavily influence the culture, it is the actions and behaviors of the employees, over time, which actually creates the culture.

For example, suppose an organization is led by an executive leadership team that has a solid work ethic. These leaders may come to work early in the morning, work through their lunch hour and stay as late as 8:00 or 9:00 pm designing the future of the organization. To them, time is important and they have what many would consider to be a solid work ethic.

Now suppose a facilities manager at one of the locations does not consider time management all that important. He often shows up 10 minutes late in the morning, arrives back from lunch later than the required time and sometimes leaves early to pick his child up from school. Employees who report to this manager watch to see what the consequences will be. They know about the work ethic at corporate so they eagerly wait to see what happens to the facilities manager.

Let's say, over time, nothing happens to the facilities manager and he continues to arrive late and leave early on more occasions with no consequences. What are the employees who report to this manager likely to do? Might they begin to arrive late, take longer breaks and lunch hours and leave early?

Imagine this behavior continues to take place for many months. The leadership team at corporate is talking with investors and telling them about the importance of a solid work ethic and completing projects on time and within budget but the actual behavior of the team members who are implementing the plan may be doing something different. Which one constitutes the culture of the organization; what leadership believes or what actually occurs?

It is the actual behavior of the individual workers, collectively, over time that creates the culture of the organization. The above is just one example of a **S**ociological factor that has to be considered when developing your strategic plan. Trying to implement a strategic plan in an environment that is not conducive to the strategic future can cause the plan to unintentionally, and sometimes intentionally, not be implemented on time and on budget.

Studies have shown that socially, employees with questions, thoughts, ideas and concerns tend not take those ideas to their direct supervisors, but to other individuals with influence within the organization. There are consulting firms in the marketplace who conduct internal social networking studies to determine who really has the power and ability to strongly influence the implementation of a strategic plan. When you look at the charts produced from these internal studies, it is often not leadership and many times not even management that have the perceived power to answer questions and move forward with implementation.

Always look at the social environment because that is an indication as to how the strategic plan might be accepted by the workforce, and more importantly, how the plan might be implemented.

Technological

Since this model was developed in 1989, technology has become an increasingly and significant variable each year. This advancement in technology enables organizations to implement change much faster than previously believed. Employees are used to new software and hardware updates and devices that require them to learn new ways of thinking and doing. Technology has enabled them to become more proficient at adapting to change.

In the past, leaders and employees were able to leave the office and try to forget about the work environment until the following morning or Monday. Now, technology has enabled them to be connected with your organization all the time. Checking email on our smart phones is now a common practice before retiring in the evening and with morning coffee. While technology was supposed to make our lives easier, it has increased our ability to be more engaged and productive, at least in the United States. This may not be true in some European countries, such as Sweden, where they use the technology to accomplish more with less time, according to some recent studies.

From a strategic perspective, it is recommended that leadership make the investment in technology. While technology does have a significant upfront financial commitment, it seems to nearly always generate an ROI (Return on Investment) in the long term. In fact, investing in technology that can replace employees can often pay for itself in the long run. Technology generally does not ask for pay increases and bonuses. You don't have to pay Workman's Compensation for technology and it doesn't request vacation time or sick days.

There are some occasions where technology has to be balanced with the rest of the strategic plan and the environment. For example, many retail establishments have installed self-checkout registers in order to decrease employee headcount and save money; however, the amount of shrink has increased in many establishments as unaccounted for merchandise has disappeared at an alarming rate, particularly in some of the larger box stores.

Organizational

The **O**rganizational structure often influences the social environment, culture and morale. I remember about 10 years ago conducting a client assessment of an organization that had two facilities. One facility hosted the "A Team" and had the corporate offices upstairs. This facility was very hierarchical. The shift manager reported to the manager who reported to the supervisor who reported to the VP of Operations who reported to the CEO, within the same building. Across the street, in building B, the manager made it very clear that any employee, at any level, could come up to his office and share any thoughts or ideas at any time. Ten-minute shift briefings were held, in both Spanish and English, at the beginning of each shift. Soon, the productivity level in building B was higher than at the corporate facility, where a chain-of-command was followed and the supposedly best employees worked with the help of the leadership team.

Many executives today are considering whether to "flatten" their organizational structure and remove the many barriers between the lowest-ranked employees in the organization and the leadership team or use the traditional multi-level hierarchical structure. For decades, many defense contractors, who often hired former military personnel, used a stringent chain-of-command because that is the management style most military personnel had experienced. A strong leader at the top would surround himself (historically, it almost always was a male) with a strong management team who believed in his mission and vision and that structure would permeate downward throughout the organization. This approach has been very effective and major military projects have been successfully completed using this approach.

Today, because many customers expect the latest and greatest technology to be updated and released on a regular (usually 12-18 month) schedule, technology–based companies have been exploring alternative organizational structures in order to reduce the amount of time for decisions to be made. One such approach that has gained attention over the past few years is to "flatten the organization" by simply removing many of the mid-level management positions from the reporting process, giving employees a more direct line of access to the top decision makers.

Research has indicated that over time, flatter organizations outperform those with many layers of management hierarchy.

While technology companies are more comfortable with this approach, many larger organizations may not be. I recall years ago someone telling me that Microsoft employees had the ability to send Bill Gates a direct email (without going through the chain-of-command) if they believed they had knowledge that Mr. Gates would want to know. On the other hand, I can't see General Electric Company getting rid of its 15,000 managers in order to flatten the organizational structure between the CEO and the employees of each BU (business unit).

There is a new organizational model called *holacracy* that was created in the US but used primarily in other countries. Under this approach, decision-making is driven down to self-directed work teams who work closely on a daily basis with the decision at hand. Letting go of decision-making power is not easy for many executive teams and perhaps this is one reason why executives in the US have been slower at implementing this approach while it has caught on more in Europe, especially Great Britain.

The organizational structure created can have a direct influence on the morale of the organization, level of quality, productivity, etc. It can also have an effect on whether the strategic plan gets implemented on time and on budget. Is it a good idea to cross-train employees? It depends. Sometimes cross-training is a great tactic that can directly influence customer intimacy strategy. However, if the organization does not pay employees at least an industry average wage or if it has a negative culture that results in a high-employee turnover rate, cross-training could send better trained employees to your competition.

Should you implement an employee team approach? This too depends upon your organization. A few years ago, while facilitating a three-day retreat with a large Japanese MNC, the VP for the organization was insistent upon including a module on team building. On one of the breaks I was talking with 4 or 5 of the 26 managers and asked them about their current team activities. I was shocked to hear that they not only didn't work as teams, they worked in 3 different states, in different facilities and on different shifts and these annual retreats were the only opportunities they had to even see or communicate with each other as a team.

On the lunch break, I asked the VP why he wanted a module to be facilitated on the concept of team building when this group didn't work as a team and never has the opportunity to collaborate as a team throughout the year. He responded that he had been reading a great deal about team building and wanted his people to have that skill. I asked him if he intended to make the necessary organizational structure changes required for these individuals to work as a team and he said no. They would just have to work it out.

Having a sense that these diverse individuals working different shifts in different facilities in different states would never be able to work as a team, we changed the program a bit and provided them with basic team-building skills and then sent them off to break-out rooms with specific issues and problems they had mentioned, and let them work as a team at the retreat, knowing that this would likely be their last opportunity to utilize these newly acquired skills.

At the end of first day we all met to debrief. The teams told the VP that they would never get to do this in the work environment; however, in the few hours they spent together, they were able to solve many of the issues facing their departments over the past year. So, team building did play a role in this organization, if only used for three or four hours one afternoon, but its impact may be lasting throughout the remainder of the year.

Today, because change occurs so quickly and more productivity is often expected of employees, collaboration is often required. In fact, some organizations are moving away from the team concept and more toward collaboration models. I often recommend skipping the team building aspect and consider using hot groups, but only if the culture and the environment of the organization will support the amount of self-direction hot groups require. Research tends to indicate that hot groups perform at a significantly higher rate than teams. If employees are going to dedicate resources toward collaboration, I would rather the effort be directed in an approach that might yield a higher return for the organization.

Behavioral

Knowledge about your organization includes its values, beliefs, morals and ethics. Because your leadership often is the one that establishes the social responsibility for your organization, leaders talk very seriously about the core values that drive the organization and how these beliefs are shared throughout the organization. They talk about the ethics; not only of the organization, but of the employees as well and how there is congruency between the organizational values and its employees.

Leaders should venture throughout their organization, talking with managers, interviewing employees, and sit in project meetings. After this venture you begin to make the connections. The members of your executive leadership team spend a great deal of time talking with investors and suppliers. The employees down line often do what is necessary to move product out the door or accommodate customers. They operate in the "real" world while executives sometimes view the organization in a "perfect" world. This disparity may occur as much as 85% of the time.

Philosophical

Understanding the philosophy of the organization is critical. It is the philosophy of the executive leadership team that helps establish the morals, values and ethics in which the organization believes. These basic fundamental beliefs evolve into social responsibility that is then exhibited by the employees in actions or behaviors in their work ethic and customer service.

If the philosophy of your organization is to increase sales or shareholder value, then the decisions made by your organization and the actions taken by your employees will reinforce this belief. Increasing sales or shareholder value represents end results, not philosophies. Organizations that use outcomes, goals or projections as their guiding principles, often have issues with implementing a strategic plan.

The key to including your philosophy into the strategic plan is to make sure it is positioned in such a way that it is integrated down to the lowest functional areas of your organization. If you are living this philosophy, it will be reflected in your actual behavior and ultimately the behavior of the employees.

For example, years ago a client who manufactured small, medical devices was led each day by the founder and CEO who was adamant that each machine be perfect before it left the factory. He wanted the highest quality and he wanted each machine tested before it left the loading dock. If a customer was waiting for the order, but the unit had not been tested, he would rather wait until the next day, have the unit tested and then shipped, and apologize to the customer for being late.

The factory production or operation's supervisor who often fields the calls from customers who did not receive their unit on time, had a different philosophy. He was tired of getting yelled at by all the disgruntled customers who called when their machine was not shipped on the expected date. He decided to use the promised deadline as the key to success instead of level of quality. He wanted every unit shipped on time to be at the customer's location, whether it had been tested to ensure it worked properly or not.

Over time, customers began to return their units and sales began to decrease. When the CEO inquired, he discovered that the supervisor had a different philosophy because the supervisor was the one who had to deal with the customer complaints on late shipments.

I reorganized the workflow to make sure that all employees recognize that the philosophy of the organization was that all units were to be tested or they didn't leave the building. Customer complaints were redirected back to the corporate office instead of the operations supervisor. This reduced his stress of delivering on time and he was told to concentrate on the philosophy of testing every unit.

It is very important that the philosophy of your organization is congruent with the actual behavior taking place. Many companies, such as Enron, WorldCom and others, posted strong philosophical ethical statements, but the actual behavior or actions of those doing the work may not have been congruent. The philosophy has to become part of the culture or it may have little effect on the actual behavior of those employees who are faced with decisions and deadlines. When that happens, implementation of your strategic plan may fail.

Economical

The **E**conomical component is the hub of the model. Changes in economic structures in organizations, such as a decrease in the budget due to a reduction in sales, often effects the other eight elements of the model. This can result in layoffs, reduced bonuses and decreased morale. Significant changes in any of the eight elements, such as a decrease in quality, can affect the economics of the organization, resulting in lower sales or lower profit margin.

Does the HISTOB-PEP™ model only work with for-profit organizations? The answer is no. Businesses, charities, school districts, colleges, universities, towns and government agencies all have financial budgets. There is an economical component to each of their strategic plans.

The key to using the HISTOB-PEP™ model is in the application. While **E**conomical is the hub because of its direct and indirect influence, it should not be considered the primary driving factor. Limited strategic decisions can be (and often are) made based upon overemphasis of the **E**conomical influence. Designing strategic plans should not be based solely upon the budget that has been created, but to create your strategic plan first, and then decide if a budget is available. Don't allow the **E**conomical driving factor to limit your strategic thinking by creating the parameters in which the planning must take place. Remember, **E**conomical is often an end result, not a strategy.

Political

Finally, the **P**olitical environment must be discussed. Every work environment that has two or more people working together has some form of a **P**olitical structure that has been created. Sometimes, this structure is based upon the organizational structure and those who possess power based upon their position or title.

In other instances, people gain power within the organization based upon the size of the project that they manage. In some companies, the person who controls the largest project budget has more political power. In this case, the power might reside with a PM (project manager) who seemingly has more influence than the person he reports too.

In other organizations, power resides in those who have the most outgoing personality. Often, major million dollar decisions are being made because one person with a strong personality proposed an idea and nobody wanted to have a confrontation with that person. In this instance, it does not matter what the person's title or position is; the only factor that gives the person power is a non-response from others in the room. For those who are familiar with management principles and theories, this often results in *The Abilene Paradox*. If you are unfamiliar with *The Abilene Paradox*, it is when a group of people collectively make a decision that is contrary to their individual beliefs.

Political power is sometimes assigned or assumed by those who control valuable resources or knowledge. The person who knows how to complete a complex task or knows where to find valuable information quickly often assumes political power based upon this knowledge. Imagine the political power the site selection team must have who decides where technology companies should place their next $8 billion silicon chip wafer manufacturing facility.

In terms of strategic planning, the political structure can affect your implementation process. In fact, if one member in the political chain does not like the direction of the strategic plan, communication can cease and projects begin to exceed deadlines and budgets. Soon, meaningful implementation of your strategic plan can be in jeopardy. Whether your organization is a hierarchical organization with many layers or a flat organization with few layers in the chain-of-command, the **P**olitical element must be considered. One politically savvy stakeholder can jeopardize the entire implementation of the strategic plan.

The HISTOB-PEP™ model allows the strategic planning team to view the organization from nine very different, holistic perspectives. These are key elements that if not considered, could hamper your entire strategic efforts. There are many more elements under each of the nine headings. In fact, when necessary, approximately 2,400 items are listed under these nine headings. The 2,400 items are a direct result of observations I have made of organizations or reading about strategic successes and failures of organizations over the past 15 years. It is also important to remember that sometimes items that might seem less significant can have the most impact or potential impact. Here are some examples from just one of my client engagements where the strategy was to form a strategic joint venture between a US company and a government sponsored Vietnamese company.

A few years ago I worked with a Vietnamese delegation that came to the United States to form a Joint Venture with a Texas company. Once, after a long day of facilitating negotiating sessions, I was taking an evening walk around the parking lot of the Hilton Hotel where we were staying and I observed all but one member of the Vietnamese delegation standing in a huddle, talking and smoking. To be courteous, I decided to walk by and say hello. As I approached the group, each member casually dropped his cigarette and placed his foot on it. My first thought was that they had only been in the US for a few days but had already found a source for some extracurricular activity. As we talked and they moved about, I saw that they had been smoking regular cigarettes. The next day I asked the lead translator for the Vietnamese delegation (Binh) why they had done that and his answer was surprising. In their government briefing before they left Hanoi, they were told that people in the United States didn't like smoking (this was when President Clinton and Vice President Al Gore were in office) and it was becoming socially (Sociological module of HISTOB-PEP™) unacceptable. They were instructed not to let anyone from the U.S. see them smoke or it could be seen as a weakness and used against them (Political module of HISTOB-PEP™) in the negotiating sessions. What may seem insignificant by one person may seem significant to another.

I remember around that same time a potential joint venture was taking place at the national level. When a group of German executives arrived at the corporate headquarters in the US of its potential JV partner it was faced with a "no smoking in this building" sign. The Germans were appalled, refused to enter the building and returned to their hotel. Doesn't that sound like the beginning of a good strategic relationship? It was then that smoking policies became one of the 2,400 items in the HISTOB-PEP™ model.

Here is another example from the Vietnam engagement. On the morning of the first day, following formal introductions, gift giving and the exchange of business cards, the executives for the Texas company sat down at the negotiating table and the

Vietnamese executives remained standing. As the lead facilitator, I walked over and quietly asked the lead translator what was wrong. Binh said they could not sit down because there was not a basket of fresh fruit on the table. I sent down to the kitchen for some fruit and when it arrived, the Vietnamese team members took their seats.

The proposed projects involved multimillion dollar projects so the negotiations lasted for seven days. On day two, we arrived in the conference room, the US executives took their seats and the Vietnamese team remained standing – no basket of fruit on the table. I immediately sent a runner to the kitchen and soon the fruit arrived and the negotiations began.

For day 3, I personally made sure there was a basket of fresh fruit on the table before either of the parties entered the room. As I was performing this task, it dawned on me that during the past 2 days, no one had eaten a piece of fruit. I decided to watch and see if anyone consumed any fruit on this third day and sure enough, the day ended and all of the fruit remained in the basket.

I pulled the lead translator, Binh, aside from the Vietnamese delegation and asked if I could discuss something. I told him that over the past three days I had observed the importance of the basket of fruit on the table and that negotiations could not begin without the fruit, yet no one ate a piece of fruit over the three-day period. He explained to me that the purpose of the fruit was not to eat. Socially (Sociologically) it was a sign of good luck that potential good things might come from the negotiations – much like a good harvest – if there is a fresh basket of fruit on the table during the negotiations. In this case, it was a social aspect that could not be avoided.

It is important to remember that changes in one area of an organization often directly or indirectly influence changes in other areas. A new manager may change the internal politics of an organization, causing a major change in the social environment, thus changing the behavior that is taking place. Laws and regulations in the political arena may cause an organization to invest more heavily in technology. Changing the organizational structure often changes the internal political environment, changing the social environment resulting in different behaviors taking place. A change in nearly any aspect of the organization often affects the financial performance and that is why the HISTOB-PEP™ model is so important.

The HISTOB-PEP™ model provides a holistic approach to analyzing the organization in order to consider all aspects of strategic planning as well as potential issues related to strategic implementation.

Thought to Ponder: Are you viewing your organization from a holistic perspective recognizing that strategic changes in one area affects the rest of the organization?

---

8 HOW TO CONDUCT A STAKEHOLDER ANALYSIS

Every organization, large or small, should develop and regularly update a stakeholder analysis. There are many different definitions for the term *stakeholder*. In fact, the United States government and the government of China have had several meetings and discussions over the years trying to come to agreement on a common definition for the term *stakeholder*.

The most comprehensive, and most commonly agreed upon definition of the term stakeholder in the United States, and the one that I use is:

Any entity, internal or external, that could affect your organization or be affected by your decisions.

Recognizing that too much analysis can bog down the process and limit the strategic mindset only significant stakeholders need plans. Too many parameters near the beginning of the strategic planning process can be more detrimental than beneficial. Evaluating stakeholders is a process that evolves throughout your strategy sessions. As stakeholders are mentioned, they are recorded and when that phase of analysis is ready, numerically assess them and only the important stakeholders receive brief, two to three sentence plans. This is a critical part of the plan, but I try to not make it a laborious exercise.

In fact, Malcolm Gladwell, in his book, *Blink,* indicated that sometimes we analyze too much in strategic planning. Sometimes, it is better to move from the idea phase to strategic intuition and then move forward. I have also seen situations in which too much analysis is used. I believe the term that is commonly used is "analysis paralysis". The analysis can become the central part of the strategic planning process. This often happens in school districts, at universities and other settings where there are many external stakeholders and the organization sets up brainstorming meetings or surveys to gather data from these "key" stakeholders.

While it is good to know what others think and believe, only the executive team can truly know these aspects and can contribute meaningfully to the strategic planning process. If the plan is to make external stakeholders feel as if they are participating in the process, that is ok, but in reality, they often provide little strategic planning value.

The same is true of internal stakeholders. While a management team knows the intricacies of a production line or the level of quality being delivered, they often know little of the external environment. Ask an operations manager what is happening with suppliers, which competitors are merging or going out of business, or changes in consumer trends and you are likely to receive a blank stare. It is advisable for executives to build a basic plan first then invite operational stakeholders into the process. Operational employees are important when discussing implementation of the strategic plan, but they often lack the strategic mindset and can't benchmark against other organizations or experiences during the planning stage.

If you want to involve more employees at the lower level, allow those employees to attend external association meetings, trade shows, conferences, etc. At least half of their time should be used gathering information from others who are at the show. Working all day at a trade show table might provide the opportunity to talk to a few competitors; however, each person working the booth should be provided the opportunity to walk around, observe, ask questions, gather brochures and conduct competitive intelligence. This is often the best way for employees to better understand the strategic external environment.

While recently in Boston, I dropped in on a trade show at the convention center for science teachers. I learned that science itself is no longer a singular discipline. When you talk about science in the U.S., you now talk about STEM (science, technology, engineering and math), as an integrated discipline, not just science.

If internal employees are truly going to be stakeholders who meaningfully contribute to the strategic planning process, they must have the ability to see the external environment, not just their internal environment. If not, their expertise is better utilized when planning the implementation section of the plan.

Stakeholders can be assessed in two different ways. A four-quadrant matrix, with internal and external relationships depicted in two quadrants and identification as to whether each stakeholder can have an effect upon the organization or be affected by the organization, in the other two quadrants. For those familiar with the four-quadrant SWOT analysis, this matrix would be similar. While this approach is adequate for merely identifying key stakeholders, it is not very effective for assessing each stakeholder. Therefore, it provides little in terms of value beyond brainstorming.

A more effective model is to use a numerically-based stakeholder analysis. I have created a numerically-based stakeholder analysis in a Microsoft Excel® spreadsheet to assess each stakeholder in order to know which ones require a plan. Using a simple 1-10 scoring system, a strategy team can quickly identify which stakeholders could have the most impact upon the organization, as well as those whose impact might be minimal. Since it is nearly impossible to plan for every stakeholder, criteria must be developed and then numerically assessed. After all, it would not be unusual for a small company to have 100-200 stakeholders and for larger companies to have 7,500 to 10,000 stakeholders. Most organizations do not have the time nor desire to develop management and mitigation plans for all of their stakeholders.

Even with a detailed stakeholder analysis, it is still possible that stakeholders can impact an organization in ways that are not anticipated. For example, prior to September 11, 2001 very few U.S. domestic organizations had designed mitigation and contingency strategies for terrorism on U.S. soil. This included the United States government who did not adequately assess the potential impact of a terrorist attack of that magnitude. According to the National Commission on Terrorists Attacks upon the United States (2004), "Since September 11, 2001, securing our nation's transportation system from terrorist attacks has assumed great urgency. On November 19, 2001, the Congress enacted the Aviation and Transportation Security Act, which created the Transportation Security Administration (TSA) within the Department of Transportation (DOT) and defined its primary responsibility as ensuring security in all modes of transportation. DOT then worked to strengthen security through its modal administrations while simultaneously organizing the new agency to meet the longer-term challenge of implementing security improvements that will not excessively inhibit commerce and travel or interfere with other critical agency missions".

In fact, terrorists did not numerically score as relevant in many private and government stakeholder analyses. The vast majority of stakeholder assessments did not even list terrorists as serious threats – meaning they were not even identified as potential stakeholders. This illustrates the importance of constantly tending to or updating a stakeholder analysis to ensure it is up-to-date and accurately reflects the potential actions and impacts related to each stakeholder.

The purpose for conducting a stakeholder analysis is to identify and assess any potential significant impact and then develop strategies related only to those that warrant attention. Examples of major stakeholders for a typical for-profit businesses might include employees (listed by category given their potential impact), shareholders, the Board of Directors, banks, competitors, suppliers, customers, the local community, etc. It is not unusual for large organizations to list hundreds, if not thousands of stakeholders.

Why are competitors represented in a stakeholder analysis? Some organizations like to identify key stakeholders who are partners and then share information with those stakeholders. A for-profit organization would certainly not share competitive information with its competitors. The competition has to be included because it can affect your organization and once you make a strategic decision and begin implementation; your competition will notice the shift and respond accordingly. Plans need to be in place to counter the actions and reactions of your competition.

Stakeholders should be identified and assessed from your supply chain to the base or raw material level. For example, in the early to mid-2000s, the United States experienced a housing boom. Developers and construction companies were often selling "spec houses" before the buildings were constructed and many people had to place their name in a lottery in hopes of winning the opportunity to buy a house. This accelerated building rate, combined with the construction growth in China and India, placed a strain on cement manufacturing facilities in the United States who were unable to keep up with the demand. There were only 118 cement plants operating in 38 states in the United States.

Many of the housing developers' stakeholder analyzes only listed those organizations that *directly* had an impact upon them. They failed to seriously consider stakeholders who could *indirectly* have an effect, such as raw material providers. Consequently, most did not have a mitigation or contingency strategy in place to respond to the cement shortage.

This established an emergency-like situation in some organizations and created the need to have an impromptu strategy session. It was finally decided to import cement into Arizona from Mexico under the then newly formed North America Free Trade Agreement.

An effective stakeholder analysis does not simply identify generic groups or entities. It identifies specific stakeholders who could impact your organization differently or be impacted by your organization differently. For example, Walmart would not just list *competitors* because each competitor could have a different impact upon the company. Thus, a Walmart stakeholder analysis would include Target, Kmart, Sears and even Kroger.

This is important because a few years ago Kmart suffered financially and was forced into bankruptcy by its creditors. Investor, Eddie Lampert of Greenwich, Connecticut purchased 53% of the Kmart stock and 15% of the stock of Sears. He merged Kmart and Sears in 2005 to form one major company, traded under the Sears symbol SHLD. Target is an indirect competitor to Walmart, but still a stakeholder. Suppose the average annual salary of a Walmart customer is around $35,000 while the average Target customer might earn around $55,000 per year. Even though the stores are both retail department stores, their market niche is different because of their customer demographics.

An event such as the merger of Kmart and Sears would

require a company like Walmart to revisit its stakeholder analysis. Whenever competitors merge, acquire or form joint ventures, different strategies may be required, which need to provide different actions, management and mitigation plans. It is for this reason that your stakeholder analysis should be viewed as an everyday, working document.

You might find it unusual to mention Kroger in the Walmart stakeholder analysis. However, it is important to note that Walmart has surpassed Kroger as the largest grocery store in the United States. Walmart has many stakeholders: competitors, vendors, government agencies, suppliers, unions, employees, etc. Each needs to be considered in relation to the potential impact on this strategic planning process.

Why is a micro-approach needed for conducting a stakeholder analysis? Employees can respond differently within an organization. Examples might include executive management versus new hires or union versus non-union employees. Each group could affect the organization differently and each one could be affected by the organization differently. Therefore, a generic heading of *employees* would not suffice for a stakeholder analysis.

New hires often respond differently than management and members of the executive team might respond differently than mid-level management. Consequently, a valid and useful stakeholder analysis must identify each stakeholder at the most specific functional level possible. Because this appears to be time consuming, many executives see this as an expense and they want to limit this exercise to 30-60 minutes. While all stakeholders cannot be considered in that time, major stakeholders can be identified and assessed. Planning will need additional time.

A logical question might be, *now that I have identified all of the major stakeholders, what do I do with the list?* As already indicated, many stakeholder lists have hundreds identified and would be very difficult to develop management, mitigation or contingency strategies for each of them. Your list needs to be narrowed so time is spent planning only for the most relevant stakeholders.

The easiest way to determine which stakeholders need attention is to numerically assess each one on your list. Using a Microsoft Excel® spreadsheet with formulas to assess the potential impact and the likelihood helps determine a value and indicates whether planning needs to be completed. Figure 2 illustrates two sample stakeholders and their potential impact. The most efficient way to complete the stakeholder analysis is to complete the first column by listing any and all entities, internal and external, which directly or indirectly could have an effect upon or be affected by your organization. This list may take some time to complete and could consist of many entities. Note that many stakeholders may be on the list more than once as each stakeholder could affect your organization and also be affected by your organization.

Next, it is important to identify the type of impact that could occur. In this column, column two of Figure 2, identify if the impact is likely to be positive or negative, internal or external, financial, etc. Parameters can be established that are important in terms of the potential type of impact. In Figure 2, positive or negative impacts have been used for demonstration purposes.

The third column provides the opportunity to identify exactly what a potential risk might be in relation to that specific stakeholder. It is important to identify what the *intended* and *unintended* consequences might be associated with each stakeholder. This is where the value of having a highly qualified and experienced strategic planning facilitator can have a significant impact. "What if" scenarios can be discussed. Each time your organization takes an action, it should be assumed that the related major stakeholders might respond. If the organization is not prepared for that response, it has lost the competitive advantage that was gained by the first move. A trained facilitator can ask the right "what if" question at the right time to ensure that major stakeholders have appropriate management and mitigation strategies in place.

Completing this step helps identify the potential impact that can be numerically assessed in the fourth column. Identifying the risks associated with a stakeholder should include obvious risks as well as "outside-of-the-box" thinking. For example, you may never know when your 4th and 5th competitors might merge and become your number two competitor. Thus, on a scale from 1 to 10 (with 10 representing the highest potential impact) each stakeholder should be numerically assessed. This number should be based on the type of impact and the real risks that are present or could be present. If varying responses are received from planning committee members, it is important to take time and discuss the most accurate score and enter it into the assessment.

Identifying a potential risk and related impact is only part of the equation. Predicting the probability or likelihood that a particular stakeholder might have an impact or pose a risk also needs to be assessed. In column 5 of Figure 2, the likelihood that a specific stakeholder might be impacted or cause an impact needs to be assessed. This number (1-10) should take into consideration the potential internal risks as well as other trends in the industry.

In Figure 2, when the number in the *Potential Impact* column is multiplied with the number in the *Likelihood* column, a product or *Value* is presented in the sixth column. It is recommended that a Microsoft Excel® spreadsheet be used to numerically complete the stakeholder impact. Formulas can be inserted that automatically calculate the product or Value for each stakeholder and that formula can easily be carried throughout the spreadsheet or changed depending upon how risk adverse the organization needs to be at any specific point in time. For example, if an organization is in an "effective" mode and has selected acquisition as one of its strategies, the formula can be adjusted knowing that at this point in time, the organization is willing to assume more risk in order to earn more reward. The opposite is true if the organization is being careful and operating in an "efficient" mode. The formulas will be more conservative.

It is important to numerically assess each stakeholder because not all stakeholders warrant extensive management, mitigation and contingency planning. Therefore, a numerically-based product or Value can determine which stakeholders offer the most risk or significant impact. While those stakeholders who don't rate high or significant enough can be skipped, they should remain in your stakeholder analysis because their importance might change throughout the year. Use the "sort" feature to force the most significant stakeholders to the top of your list and the ones with lesser impact to the bottom by using the "hide" feature in Excel® for those stakeholders who rank significantly lower.

For demonstration purposes only, using Figure 2, the formula might be designed to indicate that any Value in column six (Value) that is greater than "35" would constitute the need to design management or mitigation strategies. The word **PLAN** would appear in the *Plan* column. The formula might appear as: =IF(F4>=35,"PLAN",").

Stakeholder	Type of Impact	Risk	Potential Impact	Likelihood	Value	Plan
ABC	Negative	Loss of market share	5	6	30	
Widget, Inc.	Positive	Supplier bargaining power	7	8	56	PLAN

Figure 2

Stakeholders often appear in the stakeholder analysis more than once because your organization could have an effect upon the stakeholder and be affected by the stakeholder.

Using the earlier Walmart example, Walmart can have an effect upon its stakeholder, Kroger (which it has had by taking over the lead position as the number one grocery store) but Walmart can also be affected by Kroger. For example, if Kroger were to purchase the third largest competitor, Albertson's, Kroger might retain its number one position in the grocery industry. Therefore, Kroger would appear on Walmart's stakeholder analysis twice due to the dual possibility of impact. It could have an effect upon Kroger and/or be affected by Kroger.

Figures 2 and 3 also ask for the identification of potential risks associated with each stakeholder. Most strategic plans contain an extensive risk assessment. The *QuickStart to Strategic Planning*™

model uses a similar spreadsheet with an additional third analysis for detection difficulty. While an extensive risk assessment is not included in this book, most strategic plans contain a major section for risk and risk mitigation.

The Value column in Figure 3 depicts "0" due to the formula in the spreadsheet until values are entered. It serves as a placeholder; however, the Value will be updated as the first two columns are assessed. The final column heading is *Management & Mitigation Plan*. Stakeholders may impact an organization positively or negatively. If the impact is positive, such as an opportunity to get a better cost from a supplier, a management plan or approach should be developed to help ensure that the stakeholder impact **does** occur – thus a *Management Plan*. The organization could then review its strategies and see if vertical integration might be a good strategy to implement.

However, if the impact could be negative or have an adverse effect upon the organization, a *Mitigation Plan* or strategy might be developed to attempt to thwart the potential impact from the stakeholder. *Management & Mitigation Plans* do not have to be very elaborate and can sometimes consist of no more than 3-4 sentences at the most.

	Stake-holder	E/A	Type of Impact	Risk	Potential Impact	Like-lihood	Value	Manage-ment & Mitigation Plan
4.1	ABC	E	Negative	Loss of market share	5	6	30	
4.2	Widget, Inc.	E	Positive	Supplier bargaining power	7	8	56	PLAN
4.3							0	
4.4							0	
4.5							0	
4.6							0	
4.7							0	
4.8							0	

Figure 3

As the old adage states, even the best-laid plans sometimes do not come to fruition. Because management and mitigation strategies may fail, it is important to develop back-up or *Contingency Strategies*. A contingency strategy is the approach that should be utilized if the management or mitigation strategies fail. Figure 4 illustrates a chart to develop contingency strategies. Note that in the left-hand column each stakeholder is identified by a specific number, such as 4.1. This number appears in Figures 2 and 3 because *Management & Mitigation* strategies need to have corresponding *Contingency Plans*. Thus, whenever the word *PLAN* appears in Figure 3 of the MS Excel® spreadsheet, it will also appear in the same corresponding line in Figure 4 of the spreadsheet.

Contingency Planning	
4.1	
4.2	PLAN
4.3	
4.4	
4.5	
4.6	
4.7	
4.8	

Figure 4

Every organization, large or small, should develop a complete stakeholder analysis. This is true of larger, publicly traded companies who often have thousands of entities in their stakeholder analysis, and smaller companies with just 50 or more stakeholders. It is often recommended that divisions, and sometimes departments within organizations, develop a separate stakeholder analysis as well. Each executive is asked to create an individual stakeholder analysis and risk assessment.

Once the stakeholder analysis is complete, it is easier to conduct a risk assessment and then refine specific business strategies for the organization. Until all of the major players (*Stakeholders)* are assessed, it is nearly impossible to finalize strategic goals for your organization.

If major stakeholders are not considered, even the best plans may fail to be implemented.

Thought to Ponder: Have you identified your top 10 stakeholders and developed management, mitigation and contingency plans for them?

9 SWOTT AND TOWS ANALYSIS

SWOTT

Most executives and managers are familiar with conducting a SWOT analysis as part of the environmental scan. In fact, by the time most MBA students complete their program, they have developed 20 or more SWOT analyses, usually in marketing, project management and strategic planning classes. In fact, I don't think I have ever met an MBA student who had not conducted a SWOT analysis. It is an integral part of the skill set of anyone involved with managing an organization. In fact, *Market Line* even has an entire database called the *Business Source Complete SWOT Analyses* that contains 3,500 analyses of both public and private companies.

SWOT is an acronym for the strengths, weaknesses, opportunities and threats associated with a particular organization. It should be noted that many strategy experts use a second "T" in

SWOT(T) to represent trends. Usually I consider trends when working with established clients. For purposes of this book, I will discuss the traditional SWOT but I will address the second "T" for trends at the end of this section. Trends cannot be ignored. Even though much of strategic planning is about the future, there are still benefits to looking back historically in order to conduct a trend analyses.

Historically, strengths and weaknesses have been internal and the opportunities and threats, usually related to an industry, represent the external environment. In the left-hand column of figure 5, the terms *Internal* and *External* help identify the quadrants related to internal and external analyses. It has been my experience that there are sometimes internal opportunities and weaknesses related to external factors, so I minimize the significance of the internal and external considerations. For example, opportunities are classified as "external" under a traditional SWOT analysis; however, if the government is about to pass a law or sign-off on a regulation that mandates that products or services be mandatorily used throughout a specific industry, it becomes a very big potential strength for a company (assuming the organization is prepared for the increase in business that is about to occur); particularly if the company helped draft the regulation. While the opportunity may be external, it is because of the internal strengths that allow it to benefit from the opportunity.

Strategic planning is a creative process and while the charts and processes are used as guides, they must never get in the way of strategy development. A good strategic plan may not neatly fit within any specific parameters. However, a good SWOT analysis, if then converted into a TOWS analysis can help develop specific strategies.

Most organizations are able to list all the strengths of their organization. This list is generally fairly extensive as members of the organization are often reminded of these strengths, even in the sales and marketing materials. It is a good quadrant to begin the process as the participants are easily able to relate to their strengths.

Next, I like to move to the "Opportunities" category. Since strengths and opportunities are generally positive, group the two together, even though one is primarily internal (strengths) and the other primarily external (opportunities). Unlike the "strength" category that lists the strengths, this list may contain a few items that are "outside of the box" but that is ok. The ideas may fit within the box later and your competition might be thinking about the same items.

Ask your group to list weakness; this can change the entire mood in the room. Often, no one wants to talk negatively about their organization, particularly if leadership and management are in the room. A true assessment has to include both the good and the bad attributes so when you receive silence as a response, wait until the silence is so unbearable that someone finally responds. It seems like 5 minutes but in reality, usually someone states the first item in about 45 seconds. Once participants see that it is ok to speak negatively about your organization without any consequences, they will begin to carefully offer more weaknesses.

Strategically, you must then decide what do with the weaknesses that are identified. Some organizations dedicate resources to mitigate their weaknesses so the competition does not take advantage of them. Others, usually industry leaders, tend to concentrate on key strengths and generally avoid or ignore the weaknesses. This is a strategic decision that leadership must decide upon following the internal and external environmental scan.

Finally, threats to the organization are discussed. Threats have a greater impact upon your organization than the weaknesses, so it is important that your team is comfortable completing the weaknesses list. Team members often need help with this section, particularly if they are all internal to your organization. They may not recognize important external threats that could affect your organization. An external strategist with Diamond Eyes can often help you develop this external analysis. I almost always download an industry report and, if possible, download a SWOT analysis for a competitor in the industry in preparation for this client session.

Figure 5 illustrates one strength and one opportunity. The chart should be completed with as many items as possible.

	STRENGTHS	WEAKNESSES
Internal Environment	Our STRENGTHS in the internal environment are: **1.** <u>Good cash flow and reserves</u> 2. ____ 3. ____ 4. ____ 5. ____ 6. ____ 7. ____ 8. ____ 9. ____ 10. ____	Our WEAKNESSES in the internal environment are: 1. ____ 2. ____ 3. ____ 4. ____ 5. ____ 6. ____ 7. ____ 8. ____ 9. ____ 10. ____
	OPPORTUNITIES	THREATS
External Environment	Our OPPORTUNITIES in the external environment are: **1.** <u>A major competitor has lost market share and is weak.</u> 2. ____ 3. ____ 4. ____ 5. ____ 6. ____ 7. ____ 8. ____ 9. ____ 10. ____	Our THREATS in the external environment are: 1. ____ 2. ____ 3. ____ 4. ____ 5. ____ 6. ____ 7. ____ 8. ____ 9. ____ 10. ____

Figure 5

The second "T" in SWOTT represents Trends. It was added later, perhaps in the early 1970's, as sales and marketing managers discovered the need to study geographic trends, demographic trends, changes in customer behavior, etc. Although not listed in a quadrant, a Trends section is generally included after a SWOT chart in most strategic plans.

TOWS

I am often amazed at the number of times a SWOT analysis is completed, simply by completing Figure 5. Many members of the strategic planning team do not realize that SWOT is merely step one of a three-step process. In essence, conducting a SWOT analysis is little more than a brainstorming activity. It is great to identify the strengths, weaknesses, opportunities and threats but if the process ends at this stage, you will never see the future with Diamond Eyes. There is much more to this process. If you ask your employees to just do the brainstorming SWOT portion, I often recommend that they skip the activity altogether because merely listing the items will provide little value in their overall process.

It is only after the results of the SWOT analysis are taken to the next step – a TOWS analysis – that you can clearly develop a strategy. I would venture to say that 80% of the plans have only a SWOT analysis. Perhaps less than 5% contain the valuable TOWS analysis.

You can often tell if a true strategist assisted the strategy team with the analysis by whether the process stops with SWOT or contains a TOWS analysis. Surprisingly, when I inquire about the TOWS analysis, it seems that less than 5% of executives have even heard of it. Google only has 866,000 search results for "TOWS analysis". It is the hidden gem of strategic planning. The expert strategists know you can't use the results of SWOT for strategy development until you convert the data to a TOWS analysis.

TOWS is an acronym that represents SWOT spelled backwards and it is used to categorize the results of the SWOT analysis into match-pairs so strategies can be developed. Figure 6 depicts the typical design of a four-quadrant TOWS analysis. Continuing to use the previous SWOT results of having a strength of strong cash flow and the opportunity of a weakened competitor in the marketplace, you can begin to see the value of a TOWS analysis.

Suppose one of the strengths identified in the SWOT analysis is that your organization has strong cash flow and cash reserves – a great strength most of the time (but not all of the time). Now, suppose that one of the opportunities you have identified is a major competitor is currently in a weaker position than normal. In the upper left-hand quadrant of the TOWS analysis these two items are linked together (see Figure 6).

List strategies that use your STRENGTHS to take advantage of OPPORTUNITIES:	List strategies that take advantage of OPPORTUNITIES by overcoming WEAKNESSES:
1. <u>S1:O1 Strong cash flow: Weak competitor</u> 2. 3. 4. 5. 6. 7. 8. 9. 10.	1. 2. 3. 4. 5. 6. 7. 8. 9. 10.
List strategies that use your STRENGTHS while avoiding THREATS:	**List strategies that minimize WEAKNESSES while avoiding THREATS:**
1. 2. 3. 4. 5. 6. 7. 8. 9. 10.	1. 2. 3. 4. 5. 6. 7. 8. 9. 10.

Figure 6

This match-paired comparison is completed in each of the four quadrants until all possible combinations have been considered. For example, strength 1 would be compared with opportunities 1,

2, 3, 4, 5 and so on. Strength 2 would be compared with opportunities 1, 2, 3, 4, 5 and so on. This is continued until all possible, reasonable combinations have been considered.

Once the TOWS chart is completed, it is only then that the strategic planner can use Diamond Eyes to develop strategy. The match-paired comparison categorizes the database so analysis and strategy development can be completed.

The items identified in the TOWS analysis can now be converted into possible strategies. For example:

If cash flow and cash reserves are a strength,

And a weakened competitor has provided an opportunity

The strategy might be to <u>acquire</u> all or part of that competitor while utilizing some of the cash reserve.

Depicted in a formula, the results might appear as:

S1 + O1 = Possible Strategy 1 (<u>Acquisition</u>)

Acquisition is one of the possible strategies available to organizations described in this book.

The true value of this analysis is to brainstorm the items (SWOT), match-pair those that have a likely relationship (TOWS) and then step 3, design strategies. For those organizations that are not doing all three steps, your time, effort and energy are likely better spent in other areas of the strategic planning process.

While the above charts for a SWOT and TOWS analysis may be helpful to identify key data, those who are familiar with mapping or storyboarding might find those tools helpful in developing the analysis section.

For those strategic planners who have conducted only the SWOT analyses portion and feel as if it was just an exercise in brainstorming, the three-step process described above will lead from brainstorming to strategic planning.

Thought to Ponder: Never conduct a SWOT analysis without completing a TOWS match-paired comparison.

---

10 STRATEGIES

Once the analysis is complete, it is time to begin discussing the top 2, 3, 4 or 5 strategies that best fit your organization given your vision of the future as seen by your diamond eyes. I am not talking about goals or goal setting related to the future. Goals are meaningless if the wrong strategies are selected. In fact, goals are not strategies and once you begin to understand the specific strategies below, you won't see goals mentioned again until the end of the chapter.

Each week I do a random search on the Internet for the most recent strategic plans. Non-profits, government agencies, school districts and others often post their strategic plan on the web for stakeholders to see. I can often tell that a great deal of work has gone into creating some of these strategic plans, including time invested by management and external stakeholders. I would estimate that about 15-20% of these strategic plans contain **no strategies**. None! No one on the strategy team has diamond eyes.

No one can clearly see the future and how to get there.

In fact, they often don't even include a section dedicated to their strategies in the plan. Yet, the plan is titled a "Strategic Plan", is reviewed by tens, if not hundreds, of stakeholders, and approved for implementation. How can that be? What are they implementing? Without identifying the specific 2, 3, 4 or 5 major strategies, I often wonder what the management team will implement from that plan. This tells me that the executive leadership team has had very little formal training in the area of strategic planning and the only thing they really know to do is write mission, vision and value statements, conduct a limited SWOT brainstorming activity and create some goals (hopeful outcomes) without any strategies or tactics to ensure those goals are achieved.

My weekly perusal of strategic plans has also identified another characteristic. About 20-25% of the organizations have established a strategy section within their strategic plan, but they then fill it with goals and objectives. Goals and objectives should not appear in the strategy section. Goals and objectives are important enough to have a separate section of the plan dedicated to them. If goals are used at all, that section appears near the end of the strategic plan. Goals and objectives are expected outcomes or end results. In the strategy section, you are trying to make sure the right decisions are made, the correct strategies are selected and the appropriate tactics are created. If you are successful, the implementation may be successful and those goals and objectives that appear near the end of the strategic plan will come to fruition.

> **Thought to Ponder**: Make sure your strategic plan has a strategy section and make sure it contains strategies and tactics **NOT** goals and objectives.

While there are many strategies that can be used, I will only discuss about 30 of the most commonly used ones here in this book.

> **Thought to Ponder**: Goals and objectives are not strategies. They are the results or outcomes your organization might achieve if you selected the correct strategies and tactics and implemented them successfully.

Strategies drive the actions and behaviors of your organization and should appear early in your strategic plan, soon after the analysis section. Since goals are what you hope to achieve after the implementation, the goals section of a strategic plan can appear much later, near the end but before the succession plan. If I see a plan that lists goals as strategies, I assume this is an organization that did not have a strategist on the team and as a result, the organization will likely not perform at its highest potential. No one with diamond eyes is looking at the big picture.

Perhaps the best place to begin is to contemplate pricing strategies that are related to all for-profit organizations. As a general rule, there are three pricing strategies. Deciding which pricing strategy your organization should use is not a decision that should be made without careful consideration. Your decision also affects your level of quality, customer service, training, hours of operation, level of customer intimacy, anticipated employee turnover rate, and the way potential customers will likely view your organization. Remember in the HISTOB-PEP™ model, economics is interconnected with the rest of your organization so changes in one area will often result in changes in other areas. These pricing strategies will be discussed in general, and then certain strategic aspects of each strategy will be presented. The three pricing strategies are:

1. **High-cost provider**
2. **Best value provider**
3. **Low-cost provider**

Let's begin by clarifying that pricing has nothing to do with sales. Pricing is a component of the 4-P's (product, place, price and promotion) of marketing, not sales, and should be considered in relation to the overall philosophy and values of your organization. Items such as quality, customer service, training, etc., as related to the pricing choice has little to do with sales, and more to do with how the organization wants to be viewed by leadership.

For example, if your organization intends to offer a high level of quality and customer service, you would not decide to use a low-cost strategy because this strategy normally does not afford your organization enough profit to offer a higher level of quality or customer care.

Since the recession ended in June 2009, and the "slow growth economy" or "zombie economy" has meandered forward into mid-2014, many new start-up companies have elected to pursue the low-cost position. It is true that many low-cost providers did fare reasonably well through the recession (McDonald's annual reports state that sales grew 3.1% in 2012 and 0.2% in 2013, for example). I have seen an abundance of low-cost providers enter markets that have become heavily saturated. I think, in some instances, there is less competition to be a best-value provider, and more cash flow and profit margins available. Many low-cost providers, with minimal effort and resources, could move from a low-cost provider to a best-value provider, increase prices and have fewer competitors.

If you look at the household goods/department stores, there are several that you might consider being low-cost providers: Walmart, Big Lots, Dollar Tree, Dollar General, 99 Cent Store, Sears/Kmart, TJ Maxx, Ross, Marshalls, JC Penney, Costco, Sam's Club, etc. Some even consider Target to be in this category but I see a distinct difference in the customer demographics between Walmart and Target. I would place Target in the low-end of the best-value category.

When best-value stores are considered, there is less competition: Macy's, Dillard's, Target, Kohls and Belk generally price merchandise at the mid-level. There are specialty stores, such as Jos A. Banks, that might fit into the best value category depending upon product line. There are fewer competitors at the best-value level.

And when high-cost providers are considered: Saks Fifth Avenue, Nordstrom, Barney's and Neiman Marcus, there are even fewer major competitors in the marketplace.

When there are fewer competitors utilizing the same pricing strategy, those who are high-cost providers can often charge more for their goods and services. That does not necessarily mean low-cost companies are providing lesser quality goods. In some instances, it is merely about the brand. One can purchase a $10 Timex® (low-cost) or a $10,000 Rolex® (high-cost) and they will both tell you the time tomorrow.

Is it possible for an organization to pursue two pricing strategies at the same time? The answer is generally no. Your pricing strategy, over time, becomes part of the culture of your organization internally and the brand image of your organization to external stakeholders. That is why Toyota and Lexus remain two totally different organizations.

When The Great Recession began to enter its double-digit months, a well-known national jewelry store who is a high cost provider, considered lowering its prices significantly in order to generate sales. I immediately sent a letter to the corporate office advising them not to pursue this approach unless they thought they were likely to go out of business and this was their last resort. I explained that their current customer base (high-cost customers) would likely be unhappy that product is now being sold at a lower price to best-value customers who will now be able to wear the same jewelry. A change in pricing strategy could damage the credibility of the brand.

Think of the long-term effects that could result just by changing the pricing structure. What happens when the recession ends? Do you increase the price again and alienate the new customer base or keep the prices at the best-value level and rebrand the organization and possibly lose many of the high-end customers? In the end, I was glad to see that the company decided to wait out the recession instead of jeopardizing its brand and image that it has created over several decades. If necessary, run a sale and reduce your cost temporarily, like JoS. A. Bank does from time to time to increase sales.

Decide upon which pricing strategy you intend to use because it may be one of the most important business decisions you will make. Changing your pricing strategy can be very confusing to current and potential customers.

<u>Blue Ocean Strategy</u>: Although the concept of Blue Ocean Strategy (BOS) has been around for quite some time, it wasn't until W. Chan Kim and Renée Mauborgne, Professors at INSEAD, published their book, *Blue Ocean Strategy* in 2005 that the concept became a truly defined strategy.

BOS can be used by those organizations fiercely competing in a marketplace and looking to explore and discover new horizons or expanding opportunities with few, if any, competitors. Most industries have fierce competition. Often, the best way to gain new customers is to compete heavily and take the customers away from the competition. This creates a "bloody" situation where one organization wins, another loses, and the proverbial ocean water becomes red from the battle.

I am reminded of the Verizon and AT&T commercials a few years ago where they both spent perhaps a billion dollars advertising and comparing their services. Side-by-side maps were shown of the United States with red and blue indicators marked to show coverage area. People in Verizon commercials walked around asking the now famous question, "Can you hear me now?" It was a bloody billion dollar battle for market share.

The premise behind Blue Ocean Strategy is one in which an organization attempts to operate in an area that has very little competition, thus the water is blue and opportunities abound. The competition has not yet identified or penetrated this market and the first entrant is able to compete uncontested.

Perhaps the best example of Blue Ocean Strategy that I have experienced is the University of Phoenix, an organization in which I have served as the strategy SME (Subject Matter Expert) for the past 11 years, providing advice on the development of new strategy classes. When John Sperling started the University of Phoenix in 1976, no university was marketing primarily to the demographic population that included the working adult. Sperling had a blue ocean in which to operate for several years.

Once the competition begins to notice success in a blue ocean environment, competitors begin to quickly encroach upon the blue water and compete for market share. The University of Phoenix recognized this in 1989 and decided to discover a new blue ocean and ultimately ended up launching the first major online university program in the United States.

Now that there are over 600 competitors in the online educational marketplace, it will be interesting to see what the University of Phoenix identifies as its next blue ocean.

There are disadvantages of using Blue Ocean Strategy. It often requires the utilization of vast resources for research, development and penetration of a new market place in which little to no competition has existed. There are no companies in which to benchmark performance. Often, the competition will observe the efforts, let the blue ocean leader make mistakes and then the competition will learn from those mistakes in an attempt to enter the market later and take the market share away from the BOS leader.

Perhaps no one knows this strategy better than Coca Cola and PepsiCo. By the time the United States announced it was lifting the sanctions against Vietnam, Coca Cola had already been transported into the country for years. However, within seven hours of the announcement, Pepsi was producing product on a state-of-the-art production line just outside of Ho Chi Minh. Vietnam was an uncontested, blue ocean marketplace for Coca Cola for years; now Pepsi had to work fast to enter the market and it started on the very first day.

While BOS may not be an ideal strategy for a start-up company with limited resources, for those organizations who can discover a market niche with little or no competition, exploring the Blue Ocean can be very beneficial until the competition swims out to join you.

Long Tail Strategy: If you plan to market your business online, the Long-tail strategy is another approach that has worked well. Historically, in many industries such as books, movies and music, the approach was to create a "best seller" that would be very popular at the launch and generate huge sums of money in the first few weeks. While that approach is still in place, there is now a strategy that enables content providers to continue to sell their media even after the initial sales push, and that is through electronic gateways such as iTunes ® and Amazon ®.

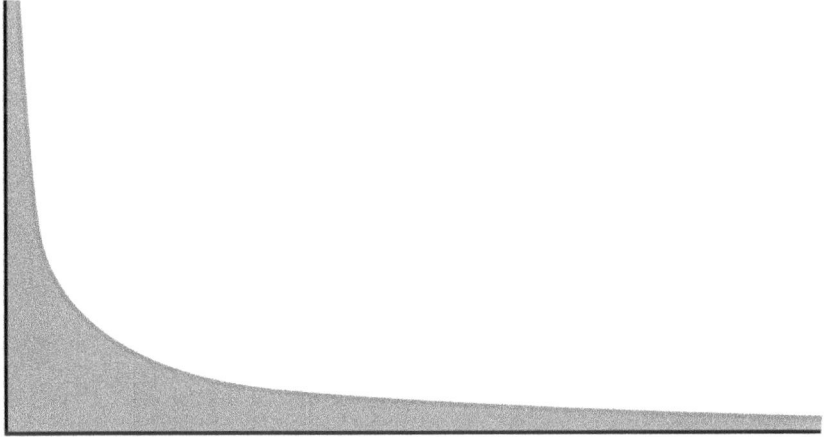

Picture by Hay Kranen
http://creativecomm
ons.org/licenses/by-sa/3.0/

While the initial marketing campaign is still designed to generate as much in sales at launch as possible, as represented by the initial peak in the chart, soon, sales begin to dwindle. It is in this long-tail portion of the chart where artists may continue to sell lesser-known or not as popular media, over time, even well-past the time when they are popular.

I believe most of the songs sold in any 30-day period on iTunes® is less than 100 copies. People may hear a song from the past and decide to download it, even though it is not the most popular song of the day.

While the strategy might work well for songs being sold on iTunes ® or movies on Netflix, can it be used for other non-media related products? The answer is yes. For example, the local car junkyard in your area now has a means (the Internet) of announcing to the entire world that it has a front grill that fits a 1988 Chevy Camaro. It may only sell 2 or 3 of them a year, but it moves them out of inventory and generates revenue as it resides in the long-tail.

Strategically, think about a product or service that is offered by your organization that used to be very popular. Is there another marketplace or opportunity to present that product or service to potential buyers? Keep in mind that sales volume will likely be low but consistent over a longer period of time; therefore, the marketing budget will be minimal. That is why the Internet is generally the best economical way to market these types of items.

> **Thought to Ponder**: How much more revenue can you generate by repositioning some of your less-selling products or services to the market using Long-Tail Strategy?

Efficient versus Effective Strategy: Many years ago, management consultant, Peter Drucker, introduced the concepts of "efficient" and "effective" into the way organizations are managed. He indicated that to be efficient means to do things right and to be effective is to do the right thing. This is a basic common management principle that most business students learn in their first management class.

While the use of this seemingly simplistic model has been used for decades at the operational level, I have noticed organizations strategically utilizing this principle in direct relation to the economy. Effective versus efficient has seemingly evolved from a management principle to a corporate strategy.

It is very difficult to be both effective and efficient at the same time. These are two very distinct principles that require different mindsets. Organizations that attempt to be both effective and efficient end up being mediocre unless they are industry leaders and can heavily invest in both strategies. In general, your organization must choose, during each strategic planning cycle, whether you want to be <u>effective</u> or <u>efficient</u> and then design tactics, objectives, milestones and tasks that match that strategic approach.

There seems to be a direct correlation between the growth of the economy and the effective versus efficient strategy utilized by organizations. It seems when the economy is growing and organizations have more resources (people and money) available, they become more aggressive, capture market share and acquire companies. In essence, they try to be more effective. However, during economic downturns, most organizations reduce head count, reduce training budgets, limit travel, and try to become more efficient because they lack the necessary resources to be more effective.

If this is a trend, strategically, economic downturns create great strategic opportunities for those organizations who have prepared to be effective, not efficient. These organizations are able to capture market share and acquire competitors at a time of weakness, instead of waiting until the economy and the competition are strong and everyone tries to be more effective.

Going back to the end of World War II, the US economy has had several economic fluctuations. On average, we typically experience 60 months of growth for every 11.09 months of economic downturn. That includes three periods where the downturn lasted 16 months or longer.

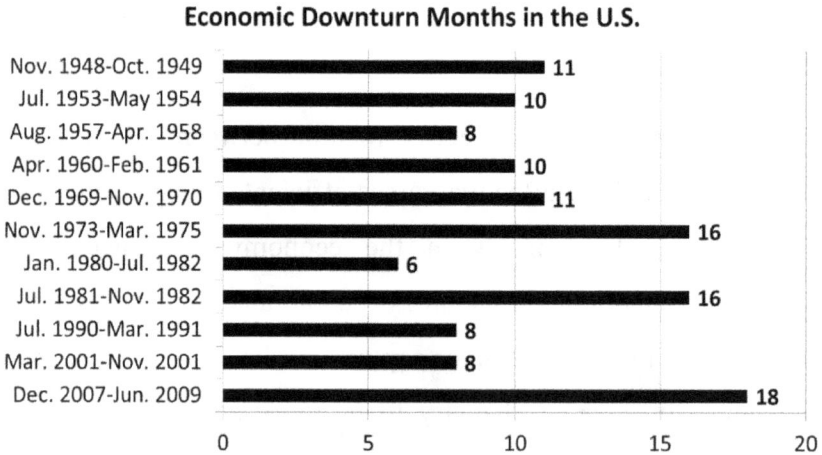

Economic Downturn Months in the U.S.

Period	Months
Nov. 1948-Oct. 1949	11
Jul. 1953-May 1954	10
Aug. 1957-Apr. 1958	8
Apr. 1960-Feb. 1961	10
Dec. 1969-Nov. 1970	11
Nov. 1973-Mar. 1975	16
Jan. 1980-Jul. 1982	6
Jul. 1981-Nov. 1982	16
Jul. 1990-Mar. 1991	8
Mar. 2001-Nov. 2001	8
Dec. 2007-Jun. 2009	18

Since the end of WWII, the US has spent approximately 10.16 years (16.5%) of the time in an economic downturn.

On the other hand, the US economy has experienced 609 months (83.5%) of the time in a growth stage. That averages out to nearly 60.9 months or 5.075 years of economic growth compared to the 11.09 months of economic downturn.

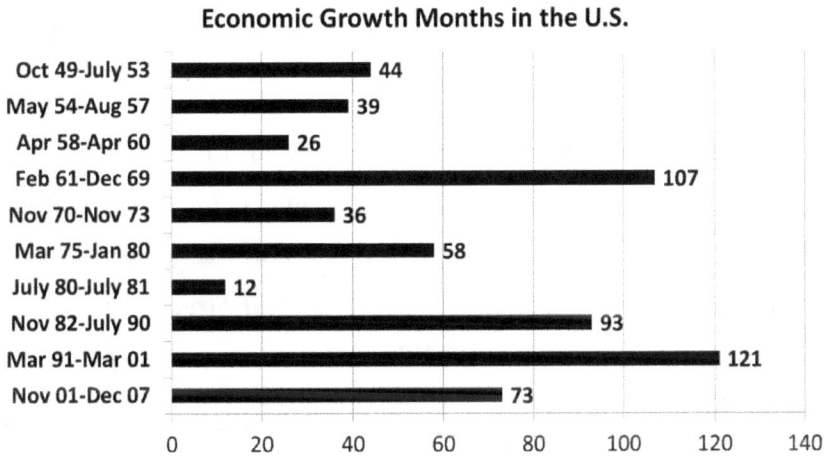

Economic Growth Months in the U.S.

Period	Months
Oct 49-July 53	44
May 54-Aug 57	39
Apr 58-Apr 60	26
Feb 61-Dec 69	107
Nov 70-Nov 73	36
Mar 75-Jan 80	58
July 80-July 81	12
Nov 82-July 90	93
Mar 91-Mar 01	121
Nov 01-Dec 07	73

In relation to the effective versus efficient strategy, these charts indicate that there are generally periods of time where organizations should strategically be very effective. In fact, the two charts collectively indicate that about 20% of the time an organization should be predominantly efficient and 80% of the time it should be effective, in theory.

Knowing when to be effective versus efficient is the key and this is why it helps to have a strategist on your team that has Diamond Eyes. Ideally, an organization should have an idea when the US economy is about to decline approximately 6 to 12 months in advance. Once you know the time frame you can begin to shift or transition from effective to efficient while capitalizing on every opportunity available.

For example, about 18 months before The Great Recession, JPMorgan Chase recognized the coming shift and began to sell off significant portions of its mortgage portfolio before the competition recognized the economy was about to not only have a significant downturn, but turn into one of the longest recessions of the past 100 years. JPMorgan was shifting from effective to efficient.

However, once the recession settled in and JPMorgan began to see the opportunities, it shifted into being effective long before the competition. In fact, as the recession was winding down, if you perused the financial pages of *The Wall Street Journal* you might have recognized that JPMorgan Chase was providing funding for probably 70-80% of the projects listed. It was taking the cash flow generated from shifting from effective to efficient and using it in a timely manner to financially gain as it shifted from being efficient back to effective.

When you think about it, on a typical day, it is difficult to earn market share away from the competition. Ideally, your organization should not only look forward to but welcome shifts and changes in the environment. It is easier to capture market share in times of turmoil than during times when it is "business as usual" and the marketplace is stable. Change means opportunity. Those leaders who have planned and are prepared are better able to take advantage of opportunities as they occur.

This may vary from industry to industry and not just the economy. There are sometimes major shifts within industries that allow competitors to take advantage of a supplier who is struggling and able to be acquired or a competitor who is struggling and lacks the marketing resources to compete in an advertising campaign.

Thought to Ponder: Be prepared for strategic opportunities and have your team ready to shift between <u>effective</u> and <u>efficient</u> with little notice and you will often earn market share away from the competition.

Differentiation: In most markets, the competition is fierce. Those organizations that can differentiate themselves from the competition have a better opportunity of increasing sales and market share. Sometimes that differentiation exists in a product or service but it can also be related to the company or brand. Differentiation strategy works best when a specific customer characteristic related to your product or a service can be identified. Once that attribute is discovered, it should be emphasized to create customer loyalty.

This strategy works well if you wish to be at least a best-value provider, if not a high-cost provider. Customers are often willing to pay a premium for that one or more differentiating characteristic, such as the unique features of your product or even your brand. In some cases, this attribute may have nothing to do with the actual product itself. The specific marketing channel that you use, your company's reputation for excellence, or the service network available to support your product or service may provide enough differentiation that the consumer will purchase your product or service at a best-value or high-cost level.

Finally, differentiation can often include an extensive advertising campaign. One of the best strategic approaches for differentiation is to use celebrities in commercials. It helps set the brand apart from the competition but this strategy can be very expensive.

Focus Strategy: Focus is most commonly used when you want to penetrate a very specific or narrow marketplace. That marketplace might be ignored by your competition or not representative of a "typical" customer. For example, a company using focus strategy might concentrate on one specific geographic area. An example that comes to mind is Stag beer, which historically had been a Midwestern beer, in the Illinois, Missouri and Wisconsin area. Its focus during the 70's and 80's was to have the beer sold in retail establishments as well as bars throughout the identified geographic area. Its focus was primarily the Midwest, near its manufacturing facility.

Sometimes focus strategy is used to penetrate a previously ignored or underappreciated customer market. Commuter airlines often use focus strategy. Allegiant Air, for example, flies into the underserved market of North Central West Virginia's Airport. An example of focus strategy might be a company that offers fractional ownership opportunities to high net-worth individuals who might have an interest or need to access an airplane on short notice.

Mass Customization: Mass customization is a strategy used when you don't want to fully utilize the differentiation strategy, but still need to service the various customers with your products and services. Up until the time of mass customization, companies often used Henry Ford's philosophy of "you can have any color you like, as long as it is black". Under mass customization, your products are altered or customized to meet the customers' needs, at near mass production costs.

An example of mass customization can be found on the KFC website for Thailand. Under the Savory Snack section, it shows one of its popular items, the Shrimp Donut. That is not likely to be a best seller in the U.S. but given the fact that Thailand sits between the Andaman Sea and the Gulf of Thailand, seafood is a staple in its daily diet.

Many consulting firms use mass customization. They have a general approach or methodology but adapt it to each client engagement. Perhaps a common, everyday example might be the local bakery at your favorite store that bakes hundreds of cakes each day but will bake a birthday cake and use any color icing and wording you request.

Perhaps one of the best examples of mass customization was Burger King's 1974 slogan that was used for 40 years, "Have it your way". It was a direct counter strategy to McDonald's "two all-beef patties, special sauce, lettuce, cheese, pickles, onions on a sesame seed bun." Burger King wanted to offer customers the ability to customize each burger for those who may not want pickles or onions, while still selling the basic Whopper® sandwich.

Operational Excellence: Operational excellence strategy is centered on perfecting the processes, systems, methods or approaches within your organization. The goal is to make very few errors, while servicing the needs of your customers. A high level of quality is often one component of operational excellence. It includes doing things right, over and over until it is ingrained in the culture of your organization.

Because operational excellence does require your constant attention and a high level of performance, organizations often strive for a lower employee turnover rate. New employees often make mistakes and need to be trained to learn the system. Given the natural learning curve, it is often better to have consistent employees over longer periods of time.

One organization that utilizes operational excellence is the Olive Garden. It tries to only hire experienced wait staff and the turnover rate at the Olive Garden is quite lower than other similar restaurants.

Of course having consistent employees on a regular basis often means paying a little more. Because of this, operational excellence is rarely used with organizations that elect to be low-cost providers. At a minimum, a best-value strategy should be used in order to generate sufficient cash flow to ensure all systems are always up and running near perfection.

Finally, organizations using operational excellence generally implement a fairly extensive training and development program. Training and development can add costs to your organization, with the hope that a return will occur as their skills are implemented. Because training and development is expensive, best-value or high-cost providers often utilize the operational excellence strategy.

If this strategy is selected, you should use it on a long-term basis. The full benefits of operational excellence are experienced over time, after the near perfection becomes part of your organizational culture.

School districts, colleges, town councils and economic development regions often use operational excellence as a strategy. One organization that successfully uses operational excellence as a low-cost provider is McDonald's. Regardless which McDonald's you enter, you can get a Big Mac with an "all-beef patty, special sauce, lettuce, cheese, pickles, and onion on a sesame seed bun". It will be the same everywhere (not withstanding global considerations).

A rare operational excellence example is used with a low-cost provider is Walmart. Its supply chain process is fully automated in order to ensure product replacement on the shelf takes place in no more than 1 or 2 days.

Customer Intimacy: Customer intimacy is a strategy in which you attempt to get close to your customers or clients by providing a level of service or quality that is customized or personalized just for them. This means you tailor or adapt your products or services to your customer needs. Amazon, by tracking purchases and even search results in order to "push" options to the customer is an example of customer intimacy.

Because this is an intimate approach, it generally does not work well for low-cost providers. It generally requires additional organizational resources in order to implement the strategy. For example, if you stay at the Ritz Carlton and you request that *The Wall Street Journal* be delivered outside your door in the morning, from then on, regardless of which Ritz Carlton you stay at anyplace in the world, *The Wall Street Journal* is part of your morning wake-up routine. Nordstrom's is another example of an organization that utilizes customer intimacy. It specializes in getting information to its customers, on an individual basis, in a manner in which the customer prefers.

Much like operational excellence, even though this strategy is mainly used by best-value to high-cost providers, there are some opportunities for low-cost providers to use this strategy. I once advised a hair styling salon to keep an index card on each customer. After each customer left, the stylist would take 2 minutes and make a note about the conversation. Noted items would include topics that seemed important to the customer such as conversations about their children, trips, work, etc. The next time the customer arrived, I advised each stylist to pull the index card and spend 30 seconds reviewing the topics and then try to work 1 or 2 of the topics into the conversation. Customers were amazed, and very appreciative, that the stylist listened and retained information from one visit to the next to continue the conversation.

Not only did the customer turnover rate decrease, but the time between visits decreased by a few days as well.

Customer Centricity: This strategy is similar to customer intimacy, but only used for a segment of the customer base. It works best with best-value to high-cost providers because the customer base is segmented and the top customers are treated differently.

With some companies, the more the customer spends, the better the relationship with the company. For example, those who fly regularly with Delta Airlines might book an economy seat and Delta might place the passenger's name on the upgrade list if a seat is available. Some customers might even get rewarded with a first-class seat, but only if they have flown regularly with Delta and earned the privilege.

Red Butler, the online virtual concierge service, offers top customers more opportunities to attend VIP events.

Organizations utilizing the customer centricity strategy have to establish the criteria that customers must meet in order to earn the special treatment. It is usually based upon sales volume and it could be offered to the top 1%, 5%, 10%, etc.

Product Development Leadership: Companies that use the product development leadership strategy strive to manufacture state-of-the-art products and services. This strategy only works with creative and innovative organizations that have the resources and abilities to research and develop new products and services quickly. Management must be able to evaluate situations and make decisions in a timely fashion. Product development leaders are often competing with themselves, replacing older products in its offerings with its latest and greatest products.

Over time, customers will recognize this strategy and will expect you to lead the way and regularly introduce new products or services. Short cycle times between products are important. Perhaps the best current example of an organization using this strategy is Apple. Its customers expect it to release a new version of the iPad and iPhone every 12-18 months, thus making its own older products obsolete. This strategy will have benefits over time, even for Apple.

To remain a leader, you must try new ideas. You must be willing to fail and fail early than wait and have the competition introduce a better competing product or service. These leaders are often best-value to high-cost providers.

Concentrated Growth: Many organizations have utilized the concentrated growth strategy of emphasizing increasing market share. Sometimes this is done by addressing quality, pricing strategies, and reviewing the amount of value their customers receive.

Generally, you would use this strategy when you want to direct the majority of your resources toward the growth of a single product or service in order to grow profits. This is usually best implemented when you use a market penetration strategy that develops your competitive advantages in a narrowly defined competitive area where you can achieve superiority over your competition.

There are three ways you can increase your sales using this strategy:

1. You can increase the number of products and services to your present market.

2. You can win over customers from your competition through excellent customer service.

3. You can attract new customers to your products or services.

This strategy works great in a stable environment that is growing. The downside of this approach is if customers' demands change, regulations affect your organization or if your products or the competitive landscape changes, you may have invested a great deal in a single approach that is now in jeopardy.

Because limited additional resources are necessary to implement this strategy, along with its low risk, this is a great strategy if you have limited funds but it works well with larger organizations as well. For example, Ford Motor Company has been able to use this strategy by increasing its efficiency and enhancing its relationship with its dealer network. McDonald's has successfully used the concentrated growth strategy for years. Walmart, Subway and Starbucks have also successfully utilized a concentrated growth strategy.

Market Development: Market development is a specific growth strategy that includes expanding the potential market in either new geographic segments, new demographic segments or new psychographic segments. It includes:

- Identifying and developing new market segments for your current products.

- Getting non-buying customers in an already targeted market segment to purchase, and

- Getting new customers in new market segments to purchase.

It is important to conduct a cost-benefit analysis and determine if it is even going to be profitable to develop and then penetrate a new market. The following four key stakeholders must be considered:

1. Existing customers

2. Customers of the competition

3. Potential customers who are not buying in the current market segment

4. Potential customers in the new market segment

Some areas that are often considered include positioning your product or service in the market, the amount of promotion required, actions and potential actions of the competition, pricing adjustments, distribution issues, product improvements and customer characteristics. Aggressive marketing campaigns are sometimes required to penetrate these markets.

By offering new, healthy menu items, McDonald's has been able to market to a different market segment. Bahamas Breeze, the small restaurant chain, might seek new locations where the demographics match its strategy in terms of pricing and selection. In existing markets, its happy hour and unique drinks, like the Bahamarita®, encourage new and existing customers to explore the menu options.

Product Development: Product development strategy involves significant changes and modifications to your current product lines or the development of new but related products that could be marketed to your current customer base. This strategy could be used to enhance the lifecycle of your current products or to enhance your reputation or brand name associated with your product or company. The premise is to sell new products to an existing customer base that is already satisfied with the product or service offerings.

An example of product development might be a new flavored potato chips offered by a well-known company such as Lays. Lays now offers over 50 different tasting potato chips. Another might be a new book by a famous author such as John Grisham to sell to those who purchased and liked the last novel with a similar theme (a lawyer) is an example of product development.

Innovation: Innovation is a risky but often necessary strategy. Organizations seeking to earn high profits and customer acceptance of new products often utilize innovation strategy.

Prior to the recession of 2007, many larger organizations were starting to concentrate heavily on product development, creativity and innovation. When the economy continued at a slow growth, even after the recession ended, many of these organizations discontinued their innovation offices.

When might you consider implementing an innovation strategy? When you believe the competition's product or service is eroding your profitability Many technology-based organizations today use innovation strategy.

Innovation strategy is often coupled with strategic alliance or joint venture strategies because of the high initial research and development costs associated with product development. That is why technology companies such as Intel often form strategic alliances with other organizations.

Innovation strategy is generally used with organizations who also have elected to be a best-value to high cost provider. Research, development and pre-marketing costs associated with innovation often mean a longer return on investment (ROI) time period.

An entire industry that was most effected by innovation strategy is the energy industry. The invention of long-wall mining totally revamped the way coal was cut and transported and today, fracking is again changing the way we acquire our natural resources. W2E, waste to energy companies are also creating innovative ways to dispose of unwanted materials and generate energy at the same time.

Finally, many new product or service ideas developed through your innovation strategy never come to fruition. Some studies indicate the success rate of creating an innovative product that makes it through research and development then pre-marketing and generates a return on investment can be as low as 3 to 5%.

Horizontal Integration: This strategy usually involves a merger or an acquisition that allows you to acquire a similar firm that is operating at a similar level. By doing so, this eliminates one competitor from the marketplace and provides you with not only the new market, but the skills and abilities of the other organization as well.

While there are many reasons why you might consider horizontal integration strategy, in nearly every instance, the parent firm acquires critical resources that it needs to improve overall profitability. Whether the reason to implement the strategy is based upon:

❖ operations

❖ geography

❖ an increase in market share

❖ the potential improvements in production capabilities

❖ the need for economies of scale

❖ the need for knowledge or resources

❖ to increase its use of efficient capital

there are usually significant potential benefits associated with horizontal integration.

In some instances, a horizontal merger can provide you with the ability to offer your current customers a broader product line. It also brings that same opportunity to the customers of the acquired firm. This is one reason why this strategy is very popular and has been very successful with technology-based companies; particularly those in the Internet security arena.

One of the primary reasons to implement horizontal integration strategy is to gain market share. It is for this reason that banking institutions have pursued this strategy over the past 12 years. Gaining market share not only means new revenue, it also means a larger customer base and fewer competitors in the market.

In other instances, horizontal integration is used in order to combine resources of two organizations in order to improve operational efficiency. Energy companies have found this strategy particularly beneficial in that regard. Often, overlapping operations can be reduced, if not completely eliminated, and supplier relationships can be integrated in order to get bulk pricing.

Vertical Integration: Vertical integration strategy involves the acquisition of organizations that supply it with inputs, such as raw materials, or customers for its outputs, such as warehouses.

Specifically, there are two forms of vertical integration: backward vertical integration and forward vertical integration. If you acquire an early stage of production company, such as a raw material provider, that is an example of backward integration. If you acquire or merge with another organization that is more directly related to your customer, that is forward vertical integration.

Backward integration is used when your company wants to increase the dependability of your supply chain or the quality of the raw materials that are used in your production inputs. This can be very effective when there are only a few suppliers in the marketplace and a large number of competitors. Not only can you better control your costs, and improve your profit margin, you can also influence the buying power of your competition. An example of backward vertical integration might be Armstrong (the company that manufactures ceiling tile) acquiring acres of loblolly pine in the Southeastern United States.

Forward integration can be used if your company stabilizes its production, marketing, distribution, and supply chain, leading all the way up to your customers. BP (British Petroleum) might be considered an example for forward vertical integration. Not only does it produce its own products, it ships it in its own trucks and then sales it at its own stations.

Concentric Diversification: Concentric diversification involves the acquisition of a business that is not a competitor, but a company related to your company in terms of technology, markets, products, or services. The new organization is usually highly compatible with your current line of business. Ideally, this relationship should occur when the combined company profits increases the strengths and opportunities of your organization and decreases your weaknesses and exposure to risk.

An example of concentric diversification might be a wedding planning firm that acquires a local florist shop. A local travel agency acquiring a tour group in another country could be considered concentric diversification.

Conglomerate Diversification: Conglomerate diversification is a strategy used primarily when you are seeking a financial return as your primary motivator. Unlike concentric diversification, conglomerate diversification does not attempt to strategically align products, suppliers, distribution channels etc. It is almost purely a financial transaction to create a balanced portfolio. Currently a large India company wants to acquire a U.S. company in the waste-to-energy (W2E) market for its portfolio. It currently sells soap.

With conglomerate diversification, the one measure of success most commonly used is profit margin. Many of these acquisitions struggle when conflicting cultures, management styles and operational procedures become too cumbersome to manage and the profit is not realized. The key to success is to continue to nurture the newly integrated entity into the overall corporate culture.

Turnaround: Turnaround is a retrenchment strategy that can be used when your company discovers that it has declining profits. It is believed, that if a company reduces its cost and/or reduces its assets, it will be able to turn itself around.

Too often cost reduction is considered before asset reduction. Since employees are often viewed as very expensive to most organizations, headcount is one of the first areas considered as part of the cost reduction. Whether it is through a healthy attrition rate or laying off employees, the goal is to reduce the headcount of the organization. Related training and development associated with employees, along with travel budgets, are also reduced under a turnaround strategy.

Assets are generally considered phase 2 of a turnaround situation. These can include the land, buildings and equipment associated with your company. Because the remaining employees still need a place to work, asset reduction is considered secondary to cost reduction activities such as laying off employees.

It should be noted that this strategy is usually most effective when a company conducts a root cause analysis and determines why it has declining performance. If this is not addressed, your company could still continue to struggle.

Divestiture: This occurs when a major component of your company is sold. Sometimes this is a particular company in the portfolio, or a division within the organization. Closing a particular business unit is also considered divestiture. Sometimes it is determined that that part of the organization is no longer part of the core competency and by divesting that portion of the organization; the remaining business unit is more competitive. Darden recently sold Red Lobster from its portfolio in order to concentrate on its efforts with the Olive Garden.

In general, a divestiture occurs when one part of the organization no longer fits with the vision or mission of your company and management believes it can be more competitive by divesting itself of that portion often as a means to gain cash. Too often this results in the loss of market share. HP's consideration of selling the computer portion of its portfolio in order to concentrate on the printing business is an example of divestiture.

Liquidation: Unlike divestiture, liquidation occurs when a company sells off its parts for their tangible asset value, not as a going concern. Failure is acknowledged and it is realized that holding on to some assets minimizes the overall losses for its stockholders over time. It is usually a step removed from bankruptcy as the company tries to liquidate its assets as a means of generating the greatest possible return possible. National furniture stores sometimes liquidate select locations in some areas where sales have been less than expected.

Bankruptcy: This generally refers to a business failure. Nearly 75% of bankruptcy filings (Chapter 7) result in a company being liquidated and closing its doors. Twenty-five percent of the time, reorganization bankruptcy (Chapter 11) is filed and creditors are asked to temporarily freeze their claims as the company makes an attempt to create a new strategic plan and restructure the organization. A filing for bankruptcy generally means the company has experienced a failure at the leadership level. Strategic decisions were made in areas where a reasonable return-on-investment did not materialize or the organization simply was not able to compete. Strategists who do not have diamond eyes may have to utilize this strategy.

Joint Ventures: Sometimes two or more organizations decide to combine necessary resources in order to compete in a particular environment. When that occurs, the organizations form a joint venture. The joint venture is owned and operated by both organizations who agree to cooperate and provide the necessary funding, resources and capacities for the joint venture to be a success. While this form of strategic relationship has become very popular since the mid-1990s, it should be noted that many U.S. managers don't like joint venture arrangements. They recognize that the JV presents new opportunities, but they are often limited in their ability to control and monitor the overall operation of the combined organization, as they are now merely a partner.

While joint ventures are not that popular in the United States, they are quite popular throughout Asia. In fact, firms in India have seemingly drifted away from seeking licensed technology agreements, and prefer to have joint venture agreements with their foreign partners. One of the easiest ways to enter the Chinese marketplace is to form a joint venture with an already established Chinese company.

There are some risks involved in joint ventures. Both parties have both financial and nonfinancial investments in the agreement but neither has full control over the operation. The failure rate of joint ventures can be as high as 70%. However, for those joint ventures that work, the organizations are often able to capture significant market share and revenue. Joint ventures are frequently utilized when one party believes it can gain a competitive advantage more quickly by strategically aligning with a partner who can assume some of the risks, responsibilities and rewards.

Strategic Alliances: Although not utilized much in the United States beyond that of technology companies, alliances can be a very successful strategy to penetrate a new marketplace or to simply learn more about another organization. It does so by limiting or mitigating many of the risks associated with JV's because each partner is able to control its own assets.

Unlike a joint venture, where both organizations have to make a significant financial contribution to the new endeavor, strategic alliances are more collaborative in nature. Generally, both sides control and utilize their own resources to move the strategic alliance forward, rather than having to dedicate the resources to a joint venture. There are no equity positions in a strategic alliance, unlike that of a joint venture. The best way to view a strategic alliance is to consider it a partnership that will exist for a specified period of time and for specified purposes and then dissolve when mutually beneficial to do so.

Joint ventures and strategic alliances should be viewed as ongoing relationships. While mergers and acquisitions are often viewed by executive teams as transactions, JVs and strategic alliances require constant care and nurturing, much like a partnership.

Outsourcing: Similar to strategic alliances, outsourcing is a business practice where a portion of the business is contracted out to a third party. This usually results in a financial savings;

particularly if an offshore outsourcing firm is utilized. Generally, the contractor agreement is written where an exchange of services takes place in return for payments. This often helps companies concentrate on their core competencies because they are now able to outsource other functions of their company that distract from their overall vision. Outsourcing also can assist companies by reducing non-core business expenses that are caused by government regulation, legislation and mandates. Issues such as high corporate tax rates, benefit packages, Social Security and Medicare are often avoided if a company is able to outsource a particular function. For example, many U.S. companies have outsourced its Sarbanes Oxley compliance to accounting firms in other countries who charge less than U.S. accounting firms.

Planned Obsolescence: This occurs when organizations build a lifecycle into the product or service. Imagine if your car or refrigerator worked forever, the manufacturers would rarely sell replacement products.

Planned obsolescence is the intentional creation of a lifecycle or lifespan of a product or service. A few years ago, while touring the Thomas Edison winter estate in Fort Myers, Florida, the tour guide indicated that there used to be a rumor that the estate had been using Edison's original bulbs up to a few years ago. Of course it was just a rumor but it promoted a conversation with a past business associate who used to work at Philips Lighting and he told me that each light bulb is built to last an approximate number of set hours. Then they need to be replaced.

<u>Summary</u>

Generally, organizations might select a minimum of two and perhaps as many as five strategies to utilize during a strategic implementation time period. Larger companies, with many divisions, might utilize more strategies depending upon their strategic environment. If companies can focus on three or four really significant strategies for a period of time, that seems to be the most manageable.

There are times when companies select the wrong strategies. When this occurs, a strategy session should be held, root cause analysis conducted, and a new strategy developed to move the company forward. Other times, environmental changes can cause a company to revisit the strategic plan and select different strategies. Government regulations often cause companies to go back and revisit their strategic plan as well.

Earlier in the book I mentioned reviewing strategic plans that are posted on the Internet each week by various organizations. Many strategy sections of strategic plans are filled with goals and contain no strategies. **Goals are not strategies!** Review your most recent strategic plan and see if your strategy section contains items from this chapter, or simply anticipated outcomes; goals. If it contains goals, your plan could have fundamental errors that might cause issues during the implementation process.

Thought to Ponder: Goals are not strategies. Goals are anticipated outcomes or end results you hope to achieve if you select the right strategies and corresponding tactics.

Review your current strategic plan and see how many of the strategies mentioned in this chapter your organization is using.

"If the only tool you have is a hammer, you are sure to see every problem as a nail."

♦ **Abraham Maslow**

11 SITUATIONAL STRATEGIES

Strategic planning is both an art and a science. While the scientific process of conducting a Five Forces analysis, a risk assessment and a stakeholder analysis are commonly used, the difficult aspect of strategic planning is developing the "right" strategy at the "right" time. This is why it is important to have a strategist with "diamond eyes" on your strategy team. What works in one company may not work for another and a successful strategy for one company today may not work tomorrow. There is no such thing as a standard strategic plan. In fact, I often tell executives that twenty people could write a plan for the same company and develop different strategies. Most of the different plans could be successfully implemented at some point in time depending upon a number of factors including the competition, the industry, the management team, the leadership team, etc.

Gauging whether a strategic plan is "good" or not can only take place once the implementation process has begun, and in most cases, can't be fully determined until the plan has been implemented and the results analyzed. The strategies have to be launched and then you can control and monitor how the customers and the competition are responding to the strategies. If sales and revenues are increasing, that might be a sign of success, but if the competition makes a counter-move (and it should), this successful strategy may have to be replaced with a different one.

Situational Strategies require your company to evaluate its past, understand its present and predict the future on an ongoing basis. This is not an easy task. Your company should not wait until the end of the year to assess performance. That may be too late. One thing The Great Recession has taught us is that the era of the annual strategic planning retreat is dead. Organizations that want to succeed appear to now have quarterly strategic planning meetings.

Situational Strategies can best be defined as follows:

When an organization compares alternative strategies under conditions in which they are likely to exist under optimal circumstances and then selects the best alternative based upon current conditions, it is using Situational Strategies.

Situational Strategies is different from game theory in that not only does it take into consideration the possible moves of the competition, but it also takes into account the possibilities of conditions or the environment associated with the strategy. It also differs from game theory because optimal circumstances are considered. For example, your company may not be ready to acquire a competitor but because of a certain condition effecting the competitor (such as a lost contract or a lawsuit), this may be the best time to acquire a competitor and the opportunity may not present itself this well again in the near future.

If this occurs, the TOWS analysis will help determine the best strategic approach. This approach requires a strategist to help align the Situational Strategies with your current mission and vision statement. Thus, your Situational Strategies must be aligned with your overall strategic objectives while still remaining flexible enough to take advantage of new opportunities. Your company may successfully be using one strategy today but a lawsuit filed against you tomorrow may necessitate changing to a different strategy.

There are several examples of Situational Strategies from the media that may help demonstrate this concept. The first was introduced earlier and that is JP Morgan Chase identifying the potential risk associated with subprime mortgages and exiting that aspect of the business before many of its competitors (also perhaps an example of Diamond Eyes). Many banks have had to write off billions of dollars in losses, while JP Morgan Chase remained fairly economically sound. Because of the situation – the state of the industry, the financial condition of some competitors and the financial state of JP Morgan Chase, it was strategically able to provide funding for many projects.

Let's review the above opportunity in relation to our definition of Situational Strategies. First, the strategic leader likely has **Diamond Eyes** in order to see the risks and opportunities. In this case, executives at Chase bank could "see" the potential fallout of the subprime mortgage industry approximately 2 years before most of the competition. In fact, on the day Jamie Dimon recognized the risk, I am told he contacted one of his leaders who was on vacation and shared his vision and desire to exit that volatile aspect of the industry. He even recognized that he would be losing short-term gains, perhaps even to the competition, but they would benefit in the long-term by making the decision to implement an exit strategy.

Next, we have to review the proposed strategies and alternatives under the conditions in which they are likely to exist, both under optimal and least optimal circumstances. At the time Jamie Dimon had his revelation, most banks had seen the opportunity to offer subprime mortgages as an optimal business practice. In fact, banks were making large amounts of money on their subprime portfolios prior to the collapse. Jamie Dimon exited the industry even while optimal conditions existed, knowing that JP Morgan Chase was leaving money on the table in the short term. They recognized that conditions may not be this strong again in the near future. It was the right strategic move at the right time, based upon the situational circumstances - Situational Strategies.

Finally, the Situational Strategies have to be considered based upon current conditions. At the time, current conditions were such that risk assessments in banks were being conducted using a distributed model, whereas in the past assigned responsibility for risk assessments were delegated to a few. Thus, under current conditions, the risks in most banks were not compiled at the corporate level. Somehow, perhaps through Operational Excellence Strategy, Jamie Dimon was able to picture the entire potential risk at hand and make the decision to sell off the subprime portfolio. He switched to a Divestiture Strategy.

Today, JP Morgan Chase has several alternatives for a potential acquisition of major competitors. Although an acquisition may not take place, even these opportunities represent Situational Strategies. For example, acquiring a competitor, along with its associated subprime portfolios, is likely still a risk today – one that JP Morgan Chase may not be ready to make. At this time, JP Morgan Chase and Wells Fargo are still downsizing their new mortgage origination side of the business (new income generation) and increasing their refinancing (lending to current customers). The banking industry clearly has not fully recovered from the recession, even in mid-2014.

If Situational Strategies exist at a time when the opportunity is not likely to present itself in the future, your company might consider making a strategic move. That may be the case in the banking industry today. This could result in a competitive advantage in the long-term, even though the risk is likely to increase in the short-term.

A checklist for Situational Strategies would include:

♦ Your ability to evaluate the past

♦ Your ability to understand the present

♦ Your company must have **_Diamond Eyes_** or the ability to "see" the whole strategy from a macro or systems thinking perspective

♦ Your company must compare alternative strategies under conditions in which they are likely to occur and under optimal conditions, and

♦ Your company must recognize if the opportunity is likely to present itself or occur again in the near future.

In today's fast-paced, changing market, each day offers many problems, issues and opportunities. This means Situational Strategies are critical to the success of your company. Should your company pursue a strategic alliance, joint venture, merger or acquisition? The answer depends upon the specific situation surrounding the opportunity – thus, Situational Strategies. For example, if your current strategic approach is to remain conservative but continue to grow at a steady pace, a strategic alliance might be a good option. If your company is in a conservative position and implementing an efficiency strategy at the moment but sees a new opportunity in a line-of-business or a new geographic area, a joint venture may be your best approach. If your organization is struggling and seeks synergy with another organization, a merger may be your best option. And if your company has free cash or stock available and wishes to take advantage of current opportunities, you may decide to acquire a competitor or a supplier.

Your organization must be able to change or adopt strategies based upon the changing conditions at the time. Those that adapt are the ones who can take advantage of the opportunities that exist.

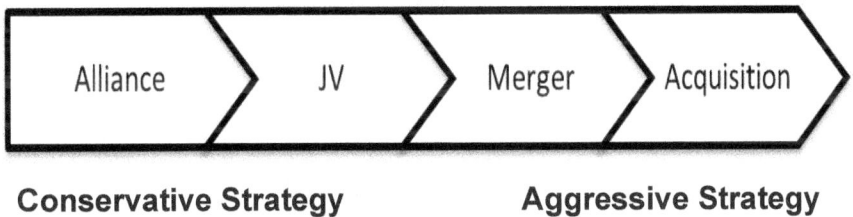

Alliance	JV	Merger	Acquisition

Conservative Strategy   **Aggressive Strategy**

It should be noted that the progression depicted above is typical, but may not have the same significance for each opportunity. For example, there may be circumstances when acquiring a company is more of a conservative approach. The strategic question might be: Which strategic option, or strategy, is best? The answer depends upon a number of factors including your company's position, your competition, the industry, trends and other factors. Collectively these all represent considerations for Situational Strategies.

In order to determine the best possible strategies, you must look at the proposed strategy from multiple perspectives. First, your strategic option should be considered in its current state, much like a snapshot in time. Your strategic option needs to be assessed using a historical perspective to see if trends support your specific approach. A strategic move must also be considered in relation to what may happen to the competitive landscape over time, remembering that time does operate on a continuum and that many business aspects are cyclical. Benchmarking the competition or using competitive intelligence may not be successful because that just identifies what has occurred or is occurring now. Strategists need to know what is likely to happen in the future.

Now that this topic has been introduced, let's explore a specific Situational Strategy. Deciding whether to acquire, be acquired, merge or form a strategic alliance or joint venture is dependent upon the situation at a specific point in time. This can be a difficult decision to make. For example, acquiring a competitor may be a risky move and may require a company to spend its available cash or utilize its credit line or stock. This might be a difficult decision for a conservative CEO, executive team or board to pursue. However, if this is the most likely time this competitor will be available for the transaction in the near future, it may be worth the risk. Only a cost-benefit analysis, risk assessment and a stakeholder analysis will help make this Situational Strategy decision.

Situational Strategies also means that strategic decisions do not exist in a vacuum. Your decisions have to be considered in their present state or condition and under optimal circumstances in order to accurately assess the opportunity. They also have to be considered in relation to future moves of the organization, competition and industry trends as well. Regardless of the strategy that is pursued, the competition will likely respond quickly so situational strategies must be considered as part of the original planning sessions, not during crisis mode.

One aspect of my consulting practice is to help US companies form strategic relationships with companies in India. Last year we introduced a US, low-cost manufacturer to seven of the top firms in India for the purpose of securing a joint venture. Based upon everything we understood about the US company, it was an ideal candidate for India. The technology seemed to match what the India companies were seeking. After the initial India meetings, three of the India firms were interested in forming a JV with the US company. What we didn't realize at the time was the US company was exploring situational strategies, one of which was filing for bankruptcy. Once the paperwork for bankruptcy (reorganization) was filed, the interest of the India firms in forming a JV with this company disappeared.

After you select your initial 2-5 strategies that you intend to utilize over the next implementation period, it is wise to identify two possible Situational Strategies that you might want to use should your internal and external situation change. Selecting one strategy to implement if the implementation process goes very well and one strategy to use if the implementation is not meeting expectations is a good approach.

In addition to the risk assessment and contingency and continuity planning taking place, this is a back-up plan for the very strategies that are selected. Remember strategies are not goals. In this instance, it might actually be possible to change your strategies and still achieve the goals that you have established. For example, a goal of $50 million in sales can be reached, even if an organization has to implement its Situational Strategy of forming a strategic alliance. Just because the strategies change does not does necessarily mean that the overall goals and objectives have to change.

Thought to Ponder: Strategies may change but goals may remain the same.

Strategy sessions or Situational Strategies involve a great deal of "what if" scenarios. The competition will generally counter any moves or strategies that you launch; therefore, you must identify at least the first counter-move or response. Prior to the recession of 2007, the banking industry was acquiring new mortgages. The industry changed and the industry shifted to divestiture strategy. Always assume that the strategies you are using today might change tomorrow.

"A sly rabbit will have three openings to its den."

♦ **Chinese Proverbs**

12 CREATING S.A.M. OBJECTIVES

Once you have selected your strategies, you can then begin to develop the objectives you hope to achieve. If the right strategies are selected, the right tactics are created to support those strategies and the right implementation team is in place, your objectives can be established hoping to lead to successful goal implementation. Now that we know the "how", you can anticipate the "what" – the goal or the end result of the implementation process and what it might look like.

One of the main purposes of your strategic plan is to design strategic objectives that are **S**pecific, **A**ctionable and **M**easurable – **S.A.M.** Your objectives are based upon your internal and external environmental scans. As already mentioned, it is often beneficial to "manipulate" time as part of your strategic planning process. It is also beneficial to develop your plan, complete with strategies with the end in mind and to work in reverse chronological order at times.

Once your vision is created and your strategies are selected, strategic objectives can be developed. It should be noted that these objectives are only the first draft and will likely be changed as your strategic process unfolds. The intent of your initial objectives is to continue to guide the strategic direction of the organization forward.

Most organizations find the process of creating strategic objectives to be quite easy. In fact, this is often easier than selecting the correct strategies. In strategy sessions it is common to hear objectives proposed such as, "let's increase our sales to $x dollars a year by year three," or "let's increase our market share by 3%" or "let's reduce the student dropout rate by 2.5%". While these proposed objectives are certainly specific and measurable, they are not actionable. In reality, these statements are not really objectives at all and are little more than outcome statements or results that the organization hopes to achieve if it selects the correct strategies and is able to successfully implement its strategic plan.

In essence, "increasing sales to $x dollars is not an objective, but the outcome or effect of achieving the actual objective. It is not actionable. Remember, S.A.M. objectives are actionable; once assigned, any employee implementing the plan knows what to do. In this example, the employee assigned the responsibility of increasing sales to $x dollars does not know what action to take. You could increase sales by simply acquiring another company that already has significant sales. Or you could introduce a new marketing campaign and spend the next two to three years implementing that plan in order to achieve $x dollars in sales. The actual objectives would then be aligned with your specific approach depending upon which strategies you selected.

This discussion regarding the design of objectives does not just take place within smaller companies. There are certainly examples of larger, and in fact Fortune 500 Companies, who struggle with the design of S.A.M objectives. I regularly facilitate high-level training classes that are filled with managers of Fortune 500 and other large companies who often struggle with this concept. In most instances, it is not their fault. They are driven by the dictates and culture of their organization and if upper management concentrates on the bottom line as the primary measure, so too do the managers down line throughout the organization. Instead of concentrating on the bottom line you should be concentrating on the actions and behaviors that need to take place that would or could lead to the creation of the financial objective or end result.

Akio Toyoda, the president of Toyota Motors Corp. (and grandson of the founder) realized this very important lesson and on Thursday, June 25, 2009 he publicly stated that Toyota needed to change the methodology used to design strategic objectives. I was very pleased to see a large corporation such as Toyota continuing to grow, learn and change an approach or process that no longer served its needs.

According to *The Wall Street Journal*, Mr. Toyoda described his strategic shift to reporters. He indicated that he intended to change the priorities of Toyota, placing products first – not sales and profits. That is quite a strategic shift for a company that is operating within a struggling industry during a recession.

Mr. Toyoda stated, "Rather than asking, 'How many cars can we sell?' or 'How much money will we make by selling these cars?' we need to ask ourselves, 'What kind of cars will make people happy?' as well as 'What pricing will attract them in each region?' Then we can make those cars".

You will learn to appreciate that by designing **S**trategic, **A**ctionable and **M**easurable objectives, your company will experience the outcomes you hope to achieve. If Toyota builds cars that customers want, it will be able to strategically sell more cars by region. And if it sells more cars by region, it will increase its overall sales. Now, Toyota can concentrate on the tactics and strategies needed to reach these objectives.

Should strategies be aligned with objectives or should objectives be aligned with strategies? This is often a philosophical discussion in strategy sessions. Most of the time strategies should be established and then objectives developed to support each of these strategies. There may be times when objectives are established and then strategies developed in relation to the objectives but more often than not, strategies should drive the actions and behaviors. For example, there may be a point in time when your company develops a macro strategy to acquire a smaller competitor within the industry. Specific objectives supporting that strategy could then be developed. As a general rule, strategies should drive the objectives. That is why this chapter on creating objectives comes after selecting the strategies.

As indicated earlier, objectives should be **S**pecific, **A**ctionable and **M**easurable. In other words, they have to be behavior-based. Each of these three attributes will be discussed individually, but in order to understand objectives from the macro perspective, these items will be discussed collectively. As already indicated, in most organizations, the complete strategic plan is not necessarily shared with the entire workforce. A strategic plan often contains too much competitive information to share with employees who could leave the company and go to work for a competitor *Note: exceptions are nonprofit, educational and governmental agencies that do not operate in a truly for-profit, competitive environment. These strategic plans are often shared with employees and the general public.*

Why would an organization design a strategy only to have an employee give a two week notice and share your strategic approach with the competition? The risk is simply too high, yet, employees must know portions of the strategic plan in order to implement it. After all, their behavior should be contributing to the fulfillment of your strategic objectives. You can make the argument that employees can be asked to sign confidentiality and nondisclosure agreements. That is true; however, if the employee can demonstrate to a court of law that the agreement is prohibiting the individual from making a living, the courts have ruled in favor of the employee in many instances.

In order to minimize the risk, each department or division is usually only given the **specific** objectives and supporting strategy (and related budget), which pertains to their business unit. The executive team that approved the strategic plan has to make sure that the objectives are S.A.M. They are also responsible for adequate resources, i.e. time, money, personnel, equipment, etc. allocated for each objective. Assigning an objective to a business unit without specific strategies, personnel and money is guaranteed to slow or stop your implementation process. Finally, someone within the business unit must be assigned responsibility to implement that portion of the strategic plan, monitor the progress and report to the executive committee.

Goals, Objectives and Milestones

You must stop the confusion within your company when employees interchangeably use terms such as **objectives**, **goals** and **milestones**. In reality, these are different terms and should not be used interchangeably. An objective is a macro or "big picture" approach that includes an action-based behavior associated with it.

This is contrary to what some theorists and strategists believe. Some will tell you that the goal is the "big picture" and objectives support the goal. I believe that is the wrong perspective. For example, *the objective is to win the war by increasing funding by $120 million this year and increase troop deployment by 4%. The short-term goal might be to win the battle today.* I believe the overall objective of the mission serves as a better guiding principle than a short-term goal. What is short-term to one person may be long-term to another.

Personally, I only use goals on a very limited basis as part of the strategic planning process. Goals are often little more than expected outcomes (earn 2% market share) or end result with little to no action or behavior associated with the goal. Using "cause and effect" would be a much better approach. That way, the concept is driven by an action. This seems better than goals with no actions or behaviors associated with them.

An adequate goal might state: ***earn 2% market share over the next 10 quarters by launching a marketing campaign in the Eastern United States with advertisements in publications designed to reach our target market (individuals 18-24 years old) while utilizing a budget of $350,000.*** This is representative of a goal that one might be able to assign to an associate and that person might know what behavior or action to take and what the anticipated end result should be. But what is the strategy? In other words, do you want to use Customer Intimacy or Operational

Excellence to ensure that you reach this goal? The long term effects could be dramatically different depending upon which strategy is selected. Goals without strategies leave employees focusing on the end result but what will happen on the last day of implementation, when they need to be constantly focusing on implementing the correct strategies?

The above sample goal is also written so management would be able to control and monitor the implementation process. But what strategy should be used? For example, if after three quarters no significant increase in sales has occurred, you might redesign your marketing campaign, analyze the competition to see if it is doing anything differently or analyze customer buying trends to determine if your goal is still appropriate. You won't know which approach is most beneficial until your company's strategies are identified. For example, if operational excellence is the selected strategy, studying consumer trends is not the best place to begin the analysis.

In fact, it seems very few goals are even written specifically enough that they can be implemented in the way that you intended. Here is a good method to test a goal. Give it to someone else and ask the person if s/he knows exactly what to do, when to do it, how to do it and what the expectation is at the time of goal completion. If the person cannot tell you how to reach the goal, for example, it is not an actionable goal. It is not a S.A.M. objective. Here is the true test: Ask the person if the goal is congruent with the company strategy being used. If the person can't answer that, a critical step has been left out of the equation.

Thought to Ponder: Goals and objectives should be
strategically aligned.

Here is a better way to define the inconsequentiality of a goal. Suppose the goal of an athlete is to make the Olympic team. That is the stated goal. It is believed that most athletes must train, on average, about 10,000 hours to perfect their skills well enough to make an Olympic team. It is also true that most athletes don't know if their goal of making the team is achieved until 1-3 weeks before the Olympics begin.

So what do the athletes concentrate on for the four years and 10,000 hours of training? The goal? No! They set the goal, and only use it for progress monitoring. Now they have to concentrate on their action-based strategies and tactics. They need to worry about operational excellence to make sure they are perfect in their performance. They need to form alliances with organizations to help support their efforts. As time progresses they forget about that goal they set many, many months ago and they concentrate on their behavior. They eat the right foods, get plenty of rest, do repetitions, build strength and stamina, etc. Then, as the last month before the Olympics rolls around, they learn if their goal is achieved – they are either selected or not selected for the Olympic team.

Thought to Ponder: Organizations concentrate too much on goals. Look at your strategic plan and if it contains a list of goals but does not identify the strategies of the organization and the tactics to be implemented how will your team implement the plan?

The other difficulty regarding goals is determining if they are long-term or short-term. What is "long-term" and what is "short-term"? To a technology company, eighteen months might be long-term whereas a manufacturer may view long-term as 3 or 5 years or more. Boeing might consider long-term goals to be 10-12 years and Apple might view long-term goals to be 24-36 months. So, the terms "long- and short-term goals" are much like art – they are in the eye of the beholder. That leaves too much ambiguity in the strategic planning process. A strategic plan should be a road map with specific stops or milestones that are reachable with a clearly defined end result or destination, driven by your strategy.

It is for the above reasons that I do not like to use the terms "long-term goals" and "short-term goals" in the strategic planning process. I recommend supporting the objectives with specific milestones – significant events that are achieved as a direct result of some action or actions such as the completion of tasks and subtasks. Here is a hierarchy that I have found to work well with strategic planning.

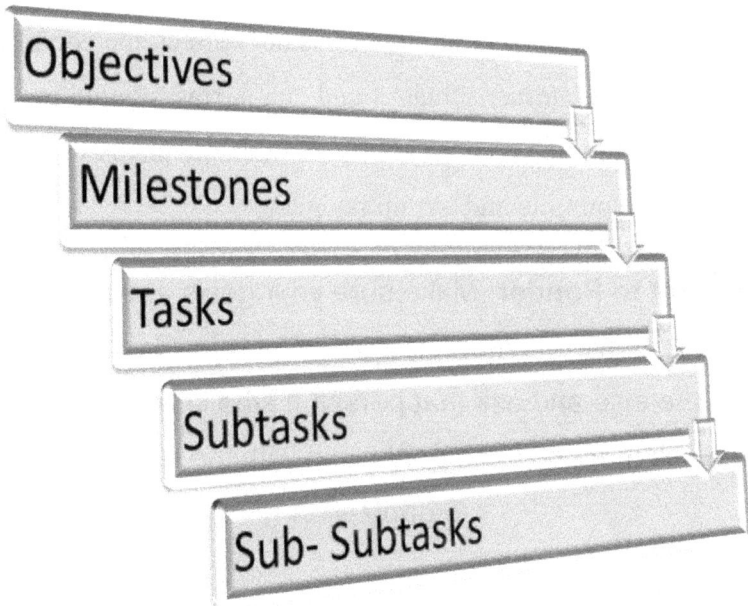

The above represents a behavior-based hierarchical model that directly leads from strategic objectives, into strategic implementation with sub-subtasks. Tasks, subtasks and sub-subtasks are specific actions that can be assigned to individuals to help ensure that the implementation process takes place. They can also be assigned to individuals or work teams and entered into a Gantt chart with start and end dates so progress can be monitored during implementation. Objectives and milestones are major accomplishments that upper management or leadership can use to control and monitor the implementation process. However, in order to be successful, you have to begin with the "right" objectives and those objectives have to be **S**pecific, **A**ctionable and **M**easurable.

And to establish the right objectives, you have to select the right strategies. If the objective or strategy is not correct, the completion of the milestones, tasks, subtasks and sub-subtasks could result in an unsuccessful implementation of your strategic plan, even if they are completed on time and within budget.

> **Thought to Ponder**: Make sure your goals and objectives are Specific, Attainable and Measurable. Give them to someone else and ask that person if s/he knows what to do. Then ask them how the goal fits in with the strategy of your organization.

13 IMPLEMENTING IT ALL

Strategic Planning is critical to your success. It is the roadmap that your leadership team designs that creates the future of your company. Unfortunately, most strategic plans have flaws in them from the very beginning. Some plans have goals posted where strategies belong. Leadership fails to recognize that goals are outcomes that occur when the right strategies and tactics are selected. Still other plans don't contain any strategies at all.

Not only should organizations have a strategic plan, the plan should contain a specific vision of what leadership wants the future to look like. On the final day of implementation when your vision is achieved, the vision statement then becomes your mission statement. It is now who you are and what you do. Your new vision statement and a new future are created.

Every organization should have a strategist on its team. That person should be someone highly experienced in strategic planning. While most organizations only plan strategically once a year, an external strategist often works on multiple plans, offering new experiences for each one. Ideally, your strategist should have Diamond Eyes. S/He should be able to look at the future, your organization, your industry, and your competition - the entire external environment.

It is important that your organization look at your strategic plan not as a process, but as a creative endeavor to map out the future of your organization. When your team has a strategic mindset, a whole new vision is created. Using reverse chronological order can create ideas that you might never have discovered had you simply started the strategic planning process from day one and moved forward.

In order to encourage you and your leadership team to utilize a strategic mindset, go into a room alone and give yourself permission to talk to yourself, walk around, draw pictures, and design the future of the organization. Use a Strategic Soliloquy Session™ to create the future.

By creating a clearly defined mission statement, employees know why they come to work each day. It defines why your employees get out of bed in the morning to come and work at your organization. It also defines why customers visit you as well. Your vision statement describes your organization in 3-5 years. It should be specific enough for you to come into your office and proclaim, "Today, our vision is achieved!"

Many organizations skimp on the analysis portion of their strategic plan. In fact, when asked to update their plan from the previous year, some departments simply add 10% to the budget and allow leadership to design 3-5 goals that should be achieved. Conduct a HISTOB-PEP™ analysis in order to view your organization from nine different perspectives. Conduct a stakeholder analysis, complete with mitigation and contingency strategies. Assess the risks facing your organization and design mitigation and contingency strategies for those as well. Finally, complete the ever-popular SWOT analysis but only do so if you intend to continue the analysis and complete the TOWS portion.

Spend time in your planning sessions thinking about your strategies. Discuss strategies that you might like to implement from your leadership level down to the lowest level of the organization. Select at least 3 or more strategies to drive the actions and behaviors of your organization throughout the implementation process. Do not mention goals. Remember, goals are not strategies – goals are end results or outcomes that might be achieved if you selected the right strategies and tactics.

Spend time asking the question "what if" so you can design additional situational strategies. If the main strategies you have selected fail to generate results, what other strategies might you use? If your competition begins to take market share away from you, what strategies might you use? Be prepared to implement at least one situational strategy throughout the execution process.

Now that the strategies have been identified, your objectives can be created. Make sure they are S.A.M. (Strategic, Actionable and Measurable). The actionable items created can serve as the tactics to ensure that your strategies get implemented. Just remember, these are what you hope to achieve once your plan is successfully implemented.

If you have thoughts on the book that you would like to share, if you need assistance with your strategic planning efforts, if you would like to arrange a presentation or if you would like added to the monthly newsletter, feel free to contact me at any time at romeo@planning2020.com or romeo@thestrategyexpert.com.

References

Blackberby, P. (2003). *History of Strategic Planning*. Retrieved January 1, 2009, from Blackerby Associates -- History of Strategic Planning: http://www.blackerbyassoc.com/history.html

Callahan P., (2003). Organic Consumers Association. *WAL-MART, AFTER REMAKING DISCOUNT RETAILING, NOW NATION'S LARGEST GROCERY CHAIN.* Retrieved February 11, 2008, from http://www.organicconsumers.org/supermarket/060103_walmart_grocery.cfm

Cantor Fitzgerald. (2009). *Cantor Fitzgerald: support of our families -- an overview*. Retrieved September 26, 2009, from http://www.cantor.com/public/charities

CNN Money. (2004). *The Man Behind the Deal*. Retrieved February 11, 2008, from http://money.cnn.com/2004/11/17/news/newsmakers/lampert/

Isidore, C. (2010). *Recession officially ended in June 2009*. Retrieved from http://money.cnn.com/2010/09/20/news/economy/recession_over/index.htm

Kentucky Small Business Development Center. (n.d.). *Marketing solutions*. Retrieved September 26, 2009, from http://www.ksbdc.org/established-businesses/marketing-solutions/

Murphy, J. (2009, June 26). Toyota boss vows to change priorities. *The Wall Street Journal*, p. B2.

National Commission on Terrorists Attacks in the United States. (2004). *First public hearing of the National Commission on Terrorist Attacks Upon the United States*. Retrieved February 11, 2008, from http://govinfo.library.unt.edu/911/hearings/hearing1/witness_dill ingham.htm

Portland Cement Association. (2008). *Cement & Concrete Basics: Overview of the Cement Industry*. Retrieved February 11, 2008, from http://www.cement.org/basics/cementindustry.asp

Von Glinow, M.A., Clarke, L., & Stockton, E. (1995, November). Vietnam: tiger or kitten?. *The Academy of Management Executive (1993-2005), 9*(4), 348. Retrieved from http://www.jstor.org/stable/4165287

WebFinance, Inc. (2009). *Strategic Planning*. Retrieved January 5, 2009, from InvestorWords: http://www.investorwords.com/4774/strategic_planning.html

ABOUT THE AUTHOR

Scott Romeo is a business and management consultant known globally as THE STRATEGY EXPERT®, (www.thestrategyexpert.com). He created the *QuickStart to Strategic Planning*™ process (www.Q2SP.com) designed to help organizations create more comprehensive and meaningful plans in less time. He works with clients in the U.S. as the Chief Strategist for Strategic Planning 2020, LLC (www.planning2020.com) and he helps US companies enter the Asian marketplace (mainly India) through strategic alliances and joint ventures as the CEO of New Horizon International Consulting, LLC (www.newhorizonconsulting.com).

Mr. Romeo has a Master's degree in organizational management. He is a Certified Advanced Facilitator (C.A.F.), Certified Business Consultant (C.B.C.) and a Certified International Business Specialist (C.I.B.S.). He has facilitated thousands of training and development sessions all over the world. He serves as a strategy SME (Subject Matter Expert) working with client organizations as either a facilitator or consultant/advisor regarding business, strategic and project planning. He is a member of the Association for Strategic Planners. He can be reached at romeo@THESTRATEGYEXPERT.com.